If there's a hole in a' your coats,
I rede ye tent it;
A chiel's amang ye takin' notes,
And, faith, he'll prent it.

Robert Burns

VANISHING GLASGOW

Through the Lens of
George Washington Wilson
T&R Annan and Sons, William Graham, Oscar Marzaroli
and others

HEATHER F. C. LYALL

Modern Photography by **Stewart Shaw**

A·U·L
PUBLISHING

Published by AUL Publishing
Queen Mother Library, Meston Walk, Aberdeen, Scotland AB9 2UE

First published 1991

Printed by Butler & Tanner Ltd, Frome and London

ISBN 1–874078–00–9

ACKNOWLEDGEMENTS

I would first thank the keepers of the various collections of old photographs whose help was invaluable in the initial stages of research. I owe much to R. V. Pringle, Mary Murray and Myrtle Anderson-Smith of Aberdeen University Library, Douglas Annan of T&R Annan and Sons, Joe Fisher of the Glasgow Room and Ian Gordon of the North British Locomotive Archives, the Mitchell Library, Glasgow, Andrew Jackson of Strathclyde Regional Archive, Elspeth King of the People's Palace Museum, Pamela Parker and Nigel Thorpe of Special Collections, Glasgow University Library, James Davis, Special Collections, University of California at Los Angeles, David Bell of the Glasgow Herald Archive, and Anne and Marie Claire Marzaroli of the Oscar Marzaroli Archive, Laura Hamilton of the Collins Gallery, Strathclyde University, Rosemary Watt, the Burrell Collection, Isabella Deans, Christine Rew and John Edwards of the Libraries and Museums Sections of the Aberdeen City Arts Department. Other individuals within these institutions were also most helpful, particularly: Jennifer Beavan, Barbara Hadley, John Annan, Liz Carmichael, Irene O'Brien, Robin Urquhart, Irene Pyle, Alma Topen, Bill Doig, Ken Robb and Sarah Allen.

The staff of various departments of Glasgow District Council were also similarly kind, especially Hugh Leishman, Sam Warnock, Jim Waugh, Melanie Ingram, Walter Gilmore; as were Drew King of Strathclyde Regional Council and Mrs Frame and Mrs Mitchell of the Glasgow Chamber of Commerce. Individuals in the business community were generous and helpful, particularly Robin Barr of AG Barr, Plc, Ruraigh Whitehead of the Copthorne Hotel, Jan Clark of Lovell Homes (Scotland) Ltd, Joe Mulholland of Mackintosh and Co. Ltd., Bill Mitchell of Yarrow Shipbuilders, Ltd, Chris Bell of Scottish Television Plc, and Geraldine Reilly of BBC Scotland. I am grateful to those who participated in the new selection of Glasgow men and women, especially for photographs and up-to-date cvs. Thanks are due to Ray Mackenzie of the Glasgow School of Art and Street Level for his advice, and to Robert Burns for his photograph of Alasdair Gray, Ronald Barclay for his father's photograph, Sarah Mackay for her photo of Stewart, Mrs Anne Marzaroli for her photo of Oscar and Mrs Elspeth Ritchie for her photo of Derek.

Stewart Shaw deserves a medal for his perseverance in attempting to reproduce the same views as his photographic predecessors. On the technical side, Mike Craig and Caroline Gilbert of Aberdeen University Library produced excellent new prints from the original GWW negatives as did the staff of the Mitchell Library from the Graham and NBLC collections. I am also grateful to Stuart Johnstone for copying original material from my own collection and the loans from Mrs Annie Mackinnon.

Finally the generosity of friends and families in Glasgow, their help and hospitality, must be mentioned — the Robbs, Bankiers, David Easton, Mrs Jessie Johnston, Anna McCurley, Carolyn Macluckie and especially John Smith, whose library and encyclopaedic knowledge of Glasgow were invaluable. My husband, Frank, kept me on course through various distractions and disasters and his help in research, photography and typing are without price. To all of them, especially the Smith family past and present, this book is dedicated.

Heather F. C. Lyall, October 1991

Prints from the early photographs may be purchased from the appropriate collections. The source of each photograph is credited alongside, and the abbreviations are :

ACAD	Aberdeen City Arts Department
ANNAN	T&R Annan and Sons, Ltd, Glasgow.
CPO	Catholic Press Office, Glasgow
GAG&M-BC	Glasgow Art Gallery and Museums — Burrell Collection
GAG&M-PP	Glasgow Art Gallery and Museums — People's Palace Collection
GH	Glasgow Herald Archive.
GR	Glasgow Room, Mitchell Library, GDC.
GUL	Glasgow University Library.
GWW	George Washington Wilson Collection, Aberdeen University Library.
S&T	Science and Technology Section, Mitchell Library, GDC.
SRA	Strathclyde Regional Archives.
SU-CG	Strathclyde University, Collins Gallery.

Other abbreviations:

GDC	Glasgow District Council.
SRC	Strathclyde Regional Council.
AC	Author's Collection.

Contents

Introduction

When **Thomas Annan** was commissioned to photograph the *'Old Closes and Streets of Glasgow'* in 1868 it was planned to replace what were then the worst slums in Europe with buildings of quality. The result tempted photographers from further afield, notably **George Washington Wilson**, to record the changes and celebrate the endeavour which thrust Glasgow to the fore in Victorian times, making it the Second City of the Empire. **James Craig Annan** continued to lead the family's business among the rich and famous; more domestic scenes captured by **William Graham**, the Springburn railwayman, have also survived.

Fifty years later, and after two World Wars Glasgow was tired. The rest of the world had caught up industrially, leaving the city without overseas markets and its people without jobs. Charles Oakley in his *Second City* (1946) told the story of the rise and fall of the 'dear green place' which had once more become a slum. Lack of wealth and poverty of ideas were reflected in the face of the city — derelict industrial sites, poor housing and an antiquated road and rail network — wistfully captured on film by **Oscar Marzaroli**.

Yet the people never quite lost heart. When vast stretches of Glasgow fell under the bulldozer to be replaced by upended coffins and the planners pushed the motorway through the centre, something stirred. Enough was enough! Glaswegians rediscovered their heritage. The Clean Air Act (1956) encouraged the civic and business communities to clean, restore and preserve rather than eradicate the past. It also permitted the Corporation to choose a parkland setting within the City boundary for William Burrell's celebrated bequest.

As with tobacco and cotton, so now heavy industries were to be replaced by different expertise in commerce and trade. Glasgow was indeed 'Miles Better' to live in and to work in, thanks in part to the despised motorway. The gathering momentum of confidence brought in its wake the Garden Festival of 1988, with attendant benefit to the Clyde Waterfront. The 1990 European City of Culture nomination gave the chance to prove to the world and its own folk that there's more to Glasgow than the Gorbals or Billy Connolly, and **Stewart Shaw** has faithfully captured these times.

The photographs of *'Vanishing Glasgow'*, taken over a period of 135 years, give a unique time-lapse record of the city and its people at work and play. If the old photos represent what has gone, let us hope that what is now recorded is *Glasgow flourishing.*

lasgow Cathedral was built on the site of the tomb of
Mungo, the patron saint of Glasgow. The earliest stone
urch, built in the reign of David I, was destroyed by
e. The present building dates from the time of Bishop
illiam Bondington (1233–58) and was completed in the
ne of Glasgow's first Archbishop, Robert Blacader
483–1508). In 1560 the Reformation compelled Arch-
shop Beaton to flee to France taking with him the
chives of the See and precious relics. Orders were
ven for the demolition of the 'idolatrous monument',
t happily the city's craftsmen assembled in arms and
ved their proudest work. In later years their zeal was
ss evident when, it is said, timber was removed from
e building to repair the quay. Only in the 18th and 19th
nturies have its beauty and antiquity received the
tention they deserve.

When George Washington Wilson published his book
on Glasgow (1868) in the series *'Photographs of English
and Scottish Scenery'* he was so fascinated by the
Cathedral that he included five photographs of it in a
slim volume of thirteen views. His photograph from the
Necropolis shows the different parts which make the
Cathedral unique: the Blacader Aisle on the left, the
Laigh or Lower Kirk which occupies the slope down to
the Molendinar Burn with the main Choir and Nave
above, and the square Chapter House on the right. Two
steeplejacks are working on the spire.

In **1990** much of Castle Street has changed. The Adam
Royal Infirmary has been replaced by James Miller's
later building of 1904–14. The Barony Free Church (1866)
has gone and Cathedral Square has been redesigned to
include a Visitor Centre.

GWW C7677

The **Cathedral** was earlier home to three congregations, the Inner Kirk congregation which had worshipped in the Choir since the Reformation, the Outer Kirk con-gregation which departed from the Nave to become Paul's, and the Barony congregation which worshippe in the Laigh Kirk until they built their own church in 179

When a larger church was built on the corner of Cast Street and Rottenrow, the **1798 Barony Church** w demolished and the entrance to the **Necropol** realigned. In the yard round the Cathedral are grave with flat tombstones, some with iron cages to dete bodysnatchers. The statue on the north of the square of James Lumsden, Lord Provost of Glasgow in 1843 ar Treasurer of the Royal Infirmary.

GWW F3174

GWW F707

The site of the **Necropolis** was formerly known as Fir Park. It was laid out by the Merchants of Glasgow as a garden cemetery, below the monument of John Knox erected at public expense in 1825. Some of the monuments are on a large scale, such as those to William McGavin, merchant, and Duncan McFarlan, Principal of the University and minister of the Cathedral, both to the left of John Knox, and in the foreground William Dunn, cotton machine maker. Other monuments of note in the Necropolis are to Charles Tennant of St Rollox and William Miller, author of 'Wee Willie Winkie'.

STEWART SHAW

Glasgow Cathedral, though Crown property, is not a monument but a church with an active congregation. To accommodate the increasing numbers of visitors, the Friends of the Cathedral have built a Visitor Centre in a redesigned **Cathedral Square**, David Livingstone's statue occupying pride of place.

GWW F1066xa

The Papal Bull for the foundation of a 'Studium Generale' to be established in the city was read at the Cross on Trinity Sunday, 20 June, 1451. The infant University was poorly endowed in its early years, meeting in various buildings in and around the Cathedral. The Arts Faculty used a modest tenement in Rottenrow, known as the Auld Pedagogy, which soon proved inadequate. The Faculty moved to the land eventually to be occupied by the eighteenth century buildings of the **Old College**. These were funded by public subscription. The buildings were arranged round two courtyards with a tall steeple between. At the time of the photographs the University had a staff of twenty-six professors and eight assistants. Among earlier staff members are found such names as Francis Hutcheson, Adam Smith and James Watt — the last surely the best-known university technician! On High Street lay the Principal's House and those of two Divinity professors. Within the College were chambers for the Regents, and Professors' Court as well as lodgings for some of the 800 students then enrolled. The first Quadrangle was mainly devoted to Divinity classrooms, reflecting the pattern of earlier days when most students were preparing for the ministry. After the Disruption of the Church of Scotland in 1843, the University 'Divines' had to be licentiates of the established church.

ANNAN

mong the rooms in the **inner Quadrangle** were those
r Medicine, Arts and Law. Sir William Thomson (**Lord
elvin**) and Joseph Lister were among the more famous
achers using these rooms. In the alcove above the
ched passage under the clock tower was a marble
ist of Zachary Boyd, a principal benefactor of the Old
ollege. At different times he was also Dean of Faculty,
rd Rector and Vice-Chancellor. The statue is now in
e Hunterian Museum.

By 1850 the University was surrounded by the worst
ums in Europe. The original merchants' houses in High
reet had been colonised by their employees as the
asters had moved west. The houses had been divided
d subdivided allowing horrendous living conditions.
etween the landlord's greed and working men's need
ere appeared no solution but plague and fire.' Sir
illiam Thomson's brother had died of typhus, which
as believed to have 'come over the wall' from the New
ennel, one of the worst of the old closes which backed
to Professors' Court. In the words of James Pagan, it

was 'not surprising that the professors should be anxious
to transfer their academic halls and dwellinghouses from
this polluted locality.' In 1864 the University accepted
the offer from the City of Glasgow Union Railway
Company to purchase the site for £100,000. The move to
Gilmorehill had begun.

Two years later the City of Glasgow Improvements
Act was passed to clear these self-same slums and
provide for new housing. The Improvement Trustees
commissioned Thomas Annan to make a photographic
record of the area before demolition began. His thirty-
one photographs of the 'Old Closes and Streets of Glasgow', 1868–77, are of major historical interest. Annan
and his sons added to the original list up to 1900, when
three editions of 'Old Closes and Streets' were available.

High Street was duly rebuilt and some of the later
buildings leading to the Cathedral still survive. The road
south to the Tolbooth is once more a building site. The
railway goods yard has gone and new developments
are scheduled.

ANNAN OG12

The **Tolbooth and Glasgow Cross** was the centre of Glasgow until Victorian times. It was the crossroads of the routes from the Cathedral south to the Clyde and east from Gallowgate along Westergait to Partick and points west. The steeple dates from 1627 and replaced the original town jail on the same site outside which in 1615 John Ogilvie was hanged as a Papal spy. He was canonised in 1976. The steeple is 126 feet high and has a clock with four faces (note the early arc lights). Originally there were 28 bells, but a newer chime of 16 small bells and a large one replaced them in 1881. The old steeple bell went to Calton Parish Kirk, and is now in the

Kelvingrove Art Gallery and Museum. The Town Hous and Assembly Rooms were joined to the prison on th west side, and rebuilt in 1814 by David Hamilton. By th time the photo was taken the civic dignitaries had move to Ingram Street, then George Square, the jail to Glasgo Green and the old Town Hall was put to commercial us Other indications as to the photograph's date are th overhead wires for electrified trams (1902) and the ge tlemen's lavatories (opened 1898). This undergrour convenience had a public telephone and was the large in the city, requiring three attendants because, unlik the others, it never closed!

In 1990 the **Tolbooth steeple** stands alone, an awkward island amid today's traffic. A competition in 1914 to ameliorate congestion resulted in the adjoining buildings being removed, but only one quadrant of the winning design was ever built.

Trongate

This early view of **Trongate** by Thomas Annan was one he included in his *'Old Closes and Streets'* produced for the City of Glasgow Improvement Trust in 1868. It demonstrates well the photographer's nightmare of capturing figures of any substance when the exposure time was so long. It was probably taken early on a summer's morning to minimise the problem and to avoid reeking lums! The scene shows the Tontine Hotel and coffee rooms built west of the Town House and Tolbooth. In 1781 a number of the wealthier citizens opened a sub-

of the Hotel. The profits were to be divided among th original nominees, the survivor winning all! The coffe room was 72 feet long and boasted a wall for adve tisements, newspapers, a logbook for the arrival an departure of shipping, and a daily delivery of ma Amazingly tobacco and liquor were barred! In the stre outside was a statue of King William III, given to the ci by James Macrae, a former governor of Madras, in 173 Alongside is an early urinal, constructed for the tow council in 1852 by W. McFarlane & Co.

rongate, 1926, captures the progress of the Keppie & enderson plan of 1914 to rebuild Glasgow Cross. The atue of King Billy has crossed the street (1898) to the bex of the island formed by Glasgow Cross Station.

In **1990** both statue and station have been removed, revealing the Mercat building (1928) and the replica Mercat Cross (1930), but power lines across the street still spoil the photographer's view.

GWW F4463

Both George Washington Wilson and Thomas Ann[an] published books of *'Photographs of Glasgow'* in 186[ ] both containing thirteen views, and in each was o[ne] of **Trongate**. GWW was an acknowledged master [of] 'instantaneous' photography, having exhibited as ear[ly] as 1859 bustling street scenes with no 'ghosts'. Annan['s] expertise lay more in portrait and fine art copying, an[d] he solved his problem of an empty Trongate (below) [by] combining a photograph of the buildings with a drawi[ng] of the street!

Trongate was originally known as St Thenew's Ga[te,] it being the way to St Thenew's Chapel, named after [St] Mungo's mother, where St Enoch's Square is today. Aft[er] a tron or weighing machine was set up at the Cross [in] 1491 the name gradually changed. Trongate was the fir[st] street in Glasgow to have gas lamps (1818), probab[ly] because of the many taverns and hotels which drew a[n] evening clientele.

The steeple of the Tron or Laigh Church stands 1[26] feet above the street. It was built in 1637 on the site [of] the collegiate church of St Mary and St Anne. It surviv[ed] a fire of 1793 when the rest of the church was destroye[d.] The replacement church is set behind the steeple an[d] now houses the Tron Theatre. The arches were mad[e] for pedestrians in 1855.

(ANNAN) GUL

GWW B1114xa

THE TRONGATE, GLASGOW. 527 G.W.W.

WW's photograph of **Trongate in 1877** looks very 'east [e]nd', with some mothers and children shoeless and men [wi]th cloth caps in the majority. The horse trams belong [to] the Glasgow Tramway and Omnibus Co. which started [in] 1872. On the corner of King Street, Fell's waxwork [m]useum proclaims 'the eighth wonder of the world'.

Annan's view of 1914 presents a more elegant Glasgow with feather-trimmed hats and straw boaters. The trams are now electric. New buildings have appeared on the corners of Candleriggs and King Street, and A.E. Pick-ard's Museum and Zoo is advertising a 'Real World's Wonder — the Elephant Man showing Alive'.

ANNAN OG8

Argyle Street looking west

ARGYLE STREET, GLASSGOW, LOOKING W. 11.304. G.W.W.

Argyle Street and hardly a woman in sight! Originally Westergait, the old route west to Dumbarton, the street was renamed for the fourth Duke of Argyll (spelling was flexible then too!) when the merchant class moved westwards and built villas on the now main road to the new Jamaica Bridge (1772). GWW shows the villas replaced by uniform ranks of warehouses, hotels and stores, including John Anderson's Royal Polytechnic whose flags are visible on the south side of the street. The original 'Hielanman's Umbrella' and horsedrawn Company trams date the photo to around 1880.

Drastic changes have followed the rebuilding of the Polytechnic for Lewis's in 1932 and the **'pedestrianisation'** in the 1980s to revive the street's fortunes as a shoppers' paradise. Following the demise of Lewis's in 1990, Debenhams are set to continue the department store tradition on this site.

Queen Street

STEWART SHAW

Queen Street, once Cow Loan on the edge of the Merchant City, was dominated by the fine arched roof of the Station at one end and David Hamilton's **Royal Exchange building** (1832). The latter incorporates the old Cunninghame mansion of 1780, solitary evidence of the wealthy tobacco lords. The Square housed for a time Glasgow's first telephone exchange (c. 1884) and the Exchange itself now hosts Stirling's Library, moved from Surgeon's Hall via Miller Street in 1954. The equestrian **statue of Wellington** by Baron Marochetti was erected in 1844 and **today** regularly gets a change of uniform! The grand warehouses with small shops below — seedsmen, tobacconists, opticians and druggists — have largely given way to chain stores and offices. **Traffic** has increased since the pedestrianisation in Argyle Street, and sadly the glass dome of the Station is almost obscured by concrete.

Buchanan Street has always been regarded as Glasgow's finest. The early mansions were soon cheek by jowl with extravagant commercial development. The city's best known stores — Fraser's, Wylie & Lochhead, Macdonalds, and Wylie Hill's — dominated the south end, with banks, Stock Exchange and other commercial enterprises dominating the north. Buchanan Street was also a magnet for photographers and the earliest of them, Thomas J. Edwards, set up at studio on the roof of the Dilettante Building (No. 49) in June 1842. The better known John Urie appeared seven years later at 33 Buchanan Street. The street boasted two Cranston Tearooms — Stuart Cranston's above the Argyll Arcade entrance, and the more famous **Kate Cranston**'s at 91, (above right) decorated by Charles Rennie Mackintosh in 1894. This was the start of a collaboration which was to provide Mackintosh with some of his best-known local commissions.

ANNAN CRM21

The street was first to be pedestrianised (in 1973) and boasts shrubs, seats and statues. The giant bronze bird created by Neil Livingstone is said to be 'the bird that never flew' from the city's coat of arms. Almost a century later **Prince's Square**, symbol of Glasgow's renewal, has replaced Miss Cranston's as the place to have a cuppa!

STEWART SHAW

hen St Enoch's Church was built astride the Square in
30 it was flanked on its eastern side by the Surgeons'
ll, meeting place for the Faculty of Physicians and
rgeons. The Hall also housed the library of Walter
rling, bequeathed by him 'for the public good'. A
ntury later the site was taken by the Glasgow and
uth-Western Railway Company who built **St Enoch
ation and Hotel**, then regarded as the 'most imposing
ucture in Glasgow'. It had 200 bedrooms and a staff of
ghty. This high standard in luxurious accommodation
s soon surpassed by the rival Caledonian Company's
ntral Station Hotel, with double the number of rooms
d staff. GWW's photo dates from the early 1880s;
nan's from twenty years later. The **subway station**
guised as a miniature castle was opened in 1896, its
vertisement proclaiming the subway to be 'the coolest
d quickest means of travelling'. Perhaps there was
l some public anxiety after embarrassing break-
wns and a crash beneath the Clyde in its first month!
he church was demolished in 1925 and the station and
el in 1977. The subway has become the underground,
h the old subway station building preserved as a
vel centre. The **St Enoch Centre**, Europe's largest
eenhouse, is home to many boutiques, familiar chain
res, and an ice-rink.

The **crossroads of Argyle Street and Jamaica Street** was the second most important in the city after Glasgow Cross. In the earliest photograph, taken from the Hielanman's Umbrella, a 'company' omnibus passes Robert Simpson's store (1851), later Arnott Simpson's. The buses, sometimes painted tartan to identify their owner, ran every three minutes on the Glasgow Cross to Ande͏ ston route. Notice the photographer's studio high up the building soon to become the Argyle Hotel. In t͏ later photograph the advent of electricity means ug͏ cables criss-cross the streets for telephones (1880s) a͏ **corporation trams** (1901).

ANNAN OG3

the 1930s the trams' upper decks are now enclosed
d the routes are colour coded. The north east corner
completely rebuilt to house the Adelphi Hotel and
ots the chemist. **Today** Simpson's has been dropped
om the store name. (The older building was recast
er the spectacular fire of the late 50s.) Across Argyle

Street Boots' blue and white glasshouse stands vacant
pending demolition since the company moved to the St
Enoch Centre. Buses and private cars run smoothly
along the tarmacadam and the overhead vista is clear of
cables once more.

STEWART SHAW

Jamaica Street

Jamaica Street was famous for its cast-iron framed warehouses, a building technique first tried in the Crystal Palace of 1851. The most impressive in the GWW photograph is Walter Wilson's Colosseum, one of Glasgow's earliest department stores. Andrew Gardner's furniture store on the corner of Ann Street is the older and more famous building. Horse and dog-carts proceed at a leisurely pace towards the bridge, and tram and gas lamps advertise soap, store, and more helpfully, street names.

In 1991 the street is **one-way** only. The large stores have gone with the exception of Martin and Frost who occupy a repainted Gardner's building.

Another street of mainly mid-19th century warehouses, the most famous being Alexander 'Greek' Thomson's Egyptian Halls, this view of **Union Street looking north** dates from about 1890. The Imperial Stores on the east side sold everything from furs to kitchen ranges! A carter transporting tea chests guides his horse along the tram rails to reduce friction from the cobbles.

Today only the street-level shop fronts have changed. The lack of traffic would indicate a Sunday, since on weekdays the photographer would certainly come to grief with the fast-moving one-way traffic system in force!

Union Street looking south

UNION STREET. GLASGOW. 1338. G.W.W.

This early view of Union Street looking south, was taken not long after the completion of the **Ca'd'Oro** building by John Honeyman in 1872. Some say the name derives from Venice's celebrated Golden House which the building tries to emulate; others that it comes from the famous restaurant of the same name of the late 1920s. The building holds special memories for many Glaswegians, for it was popular as a venue for weddings before and after World War II, only losing its crown to the Grosvenor further along Gordon Street in the 1950s. The small building immediately south of the Ca'd'Oro was the premises of John Leckie, saddler and portmanteau maker. Next door, in an original mansion, were the offices of the North British Daily Mail, who rebuilt on both sites c. 1898.

The **fire** which gutted the Ca'd'Oro building in **1987** may have done the city a favour, according to the architects, since it destroyed an ugly attic addition of 1927. Fortunately the prevailing mood of optimism found enough money to restore the building to its former glory, even adding two more bays on Union Street to create an unbroken facade. **Waterstone's**, the booksellers, now use the beautiful windows to great advantage.

STEWART SHAW

STEWART SHAW

Renfield Street from Gordon Street

GWW C7150

RENFIELD STREET, GLASGOW. SUNLIGHT SOAP 10,440. G.W.W.

AC

The view of **Renfield Street north from Gordon Stree** shows the elegant three and four storey building already blackened by soot. Just visible in the distance one of the chief culprits — Townsend's stack, built for th Crawford Street Chemical Works in 1859 and towerin twenty feet above its rival at St Rollox built in 1842, whic had been at that time one of the tallest in Europe. Shop with well-known names line the streets — R&W Fors th's, John Smith & Son, Reid and Todd and the Clydesda Rubber Company. The entire Forsyth building (with th scalloped awnings) was rebuilt in 1916 as Cranston Picture House and tearooms and is once more unde going massive reconstruction.

Renfield Street north of St Vincent Street is photo graphed about ten years later. The 'Company' hors tram now wears the Corporation livery (1894) an bowlers instead of toppers predominate. A four wheele cab or 'growler' (so called for the noise it made on th cobbles) makes its way past the City of Glasgow Li Assurance building. This was to be replaced in 1930 b James Miller's furniture warehouse, now used by th 'Pru'. The low buildings opposite here also vanished, be replaced by an earlier Miller 'monster' designed face St Vincent Street, the Bank of Scotland (1927). Th former Conservative Club, now Scottish Widows, c West George Street lost its palazzo look in 1958 and si beside an ugly Odeon Cinema subdivided in 1970 offer a variety of films simultaneously.

Renfield Street from St Vincent Street

GWW C2235

F. LYALL

St Vincent Place looking east

St Vincent Place, captured here by GWW around 1880, might be described as the commercial heart of Glasgow with the imposing row of banks and insurance buildings leading to George Square. The only building set to change was the low building on the north side beyond the Evening Citizen's clock. In Annan's view c.1914 the white marble Anchor Line offices have not yet succumbed to the all pervading soot. The photographic studio of A & G Taylor has also gone.

In 1990 the buildings have been restored to their original glowing colours. Of greatest interest in this sequence is the change in pavement furnishings — the street lights and the 'cludgie', Glasgow's first public lavatory for men. Until 1892 when this was built, men had to make do with urinals and only women's conveniences had actual water-closets and washhand basins. The iron work from McFarlane's Saracen Foundry is still in use today.

STEWART SHAW

29

George Square

GWW E4335

GEORGE SQUARE, GLASGOW. 89. G.W.W.

GWW A2985

GEORGE SQUARE, GLASGOW, FROM S.W. 10,442. GWW

STEWART SHAW

George Square was initially laid out
c. 1787 in grass and shrubbery, and
reserved for the use of citizens possessing
the surrounding houses. These were low
two and three storey buildings many of
which were taken over by hotels soon
after the arrival of the railway at the Edinburgh and Glasgow's western terminus at
Queen Street in 1842.

In the early picture by GWW (opposite
above) the hotels visible are the Queen's,
the Royal, the Crown, and Scott's Hotel
(the white building on George Street). The
eastern side of the Square is still private
dwellings. Many of Glasgow's famous
statues are already in situ. Sir John Moore
(1819) on the south side is the earliest,
followed by James Watt (1832) nearest the
camera and Sir Walter Scott's 80 foot high
column (1837). The equestrian statue of
Queen Victoria by Baron Marochetti was
moved from its first site in St Vincent Place
to balance that of Albert (also by the
Baron) in 1866.

Twenty years later (opposite below) the
Square is dominated by the recently completed City Chambers, the area of grass-
land has diminished and the Square
paved.

Ninety years later (above) the buildings
and statues are almost obscured by trees
and the northern skyline has changed dramatically, as the fireworks display to
welcome 1990, shows.

GDC

This early view of **George Squa[re]** is by GWW **c. 1867**. Looking nor[th] east. we can see Scott's hotel h[as] yet to be painted and on the sou[th] east corner the old Post Office s[tands] opposite the George Hotel. T[he] later view, **c. 1875**, shows the ne[w] General Post Office in constru[c]tion. Nearest the photographer [is] the statue of Sir Robert Peel, t[he] first of three Lord Rectors [of] Glasgow University to be re[p]resented in the Square.

GWW F4461

GEORGE SQUARE. GLASGOW. 89.

GWW E2233

GEORGE SQUARE. GLASGOW. 1346. G.W.W.

George Square, Glasgow. 10,047. G.W.W.

eorge Square in 1888 now flects the civic pride of Gla-vegians. The newly com-eted City Chambers still with mporary doors and workmen elivering materials balances e completed General Post ffice. The cab shelter has een moved to the north side the Square (cf. p. 30) and the eas of grass and trees arranged.

In **1990** the decorations nor-ally hung for the festive ason remained all through e Year of Culture.

The Annan view of **the Square looking north west** dates from around 1870. The terrace on the west side with the Crow Hotel (owned by the Cranston family) and the Clarence Hotel is in the process of change. Already the Bank of Scotland (1869) had replaced the Waverley, another hotel on that side. Later Queen Street Station acquired a splendid arched roof (1880), and the **Merchants House** joined the Bank of Scotland from earlier premises in Wilson Street (now part of the High Court). Glasgow Chamber of Commerce, the oldest in the United Kingdom has its headquarters in the House.

The North British Imperial Hotel occupied the west corner of Queen Street adjacent to the Wardlaw Kirk. It moved in 1903 to the larger site of the Queen's Hotel as the new North British Hotel, in keen competition with the other great railway hotels. It survives now as the Copthorne which still maintains traditions of comfort and good food.

GEORGE SQUARE, GLASGOW. 1345. G.W.W.

GWW D1753

GEORGE SQUARE, GLASGOW. 1345. G.W.W.

Wilson in his **view up North Hanover Street** shows a soldier and two poets have been added to the congregation of greats. Sir Colin Campbell, Lord Clyde. was thrust into the history books by the exploits of his Highland Brigade's 'thin red line' at Balaclava. It was fitting that his statue (1868) should stand alongside that of his mentor at Corunna, Sir John Moore. In 1877 Thomas Campbell, poet, three times Rector of the University, who coined the phrase 'distance lends enchantment to the view', was added along with one of Robert Burns. Statues of Sir Thomas Graham, one-time chemistry professor at the Andersonian University and James Oswald, MP, sit in the south east and north east corners of the Square. Statues of William Gladstone, also a University Rector, and David Livingstone complete the 'Victorian Valhalla'. The latter statue now more fittingly adorns Cathedral Square in High Street. On the east of North Hanover Street the **Colleges of Building and Printing** dwarf the lower George House office block fronting the Square.

George Square—days to remember

e **laying of the foundation stone of the City Cham-**
rs on 6th October 1883 was an occasion of great inter-
and pride. The photograph looking west was taken
J. Russell Stewart from a building in John Street. The
r arches mark the corners of George Square. Two
npetitions had been held before the design by
liam Young, a Paisley-born architect, was chosen for
new building. Lord Provost Ure did the honours,
een Victoria and the Prince of Wales having declined
invitation. Queen Victoria eventually came to
sgow in 1888, tempted by the great International
nibition in Kelvingrove. She visited the new City
ambers and conferred a baronetcy on the then Lord
ovost, Sir James King.
more sombre note marked the **unveiling of the**
notaph by Earl Haig on 31st May 1924. The monument
remember the dead of the Great War was intended
the architect, Sir J. J. Burnett, also to have a reflecting
ken pool between the giant lions.
Royal Garden Party was held in the Square on 1st
y 1983 to celebrate the **bicentennial of Glasgow's**
amber of Commerce. With rare good luck the
ather stayed fine, and the champagne flowed!
party of a different 'spirit' was held on Hogmanay
launch Glasgow 1990 as the **European City of**
lture. A giant stage was set up and many local per-
alities helped in the sing-along.

The **Queen's Square** is one of the **City Chambers'** many smaller rooms. Tradition has it that this was where Queen Victoria was received when she visited the Chambers in 1888. The painting was attributed to Sir David Wilkie, but may be one by Sir Daniel Macnee brought from the old Municipal and County Buildings on Wilson Street. It was removed to Kelvingrove Art Gallery in 1981 to make room for portraits of Glasgow's Lord Provosts.

The grand scale of **Glasgow's municipal buildings** is exceeded only by the lavish finish of its **interior**. All was intended to reflect the city's wealth and importance in the new industrial age.

William Young designed the building to be lit by electricity from the outset, but his central dome above this stairwell and large windows light the breccia marble almost from within and create a grandeur reminiscent of a palace.

Buchanan Street looking south to St Enoch's Church from St George's Church was taken in 1877 to show the newly completed Stock Exchange. It opened just a year before the collapse of the City of Glasgow Bank with losses in excess of £6,000,000. The integrity of Glasgow businessmen was such that the Relief Committee formed by the liquidators was able to pay back 18/- in the pound within three years. On a lighter note the businessmen had an immediate supply of things delectable from Edgars — new season's teas, light summer clarets and stores for the moors — very huntin', shootin' and fishin'! The interior of the Exchange was gutted in 1971 to create office accommodation but shops and a restaurant continue to occupy the premises at street level.

St George's Church in the middle of the Square has served the business community since it was opened in 1808. Joined by the people of Tron St Anne's from Dundas Street it has always had full congregations, and is now under the leadership of the Rev. Eric Alexander, well-known beyond Scotland as well as at home.

BUCHANAN STREET, GLASGOW. 2991. G.W.W.

The **upper part of Buchanan Street** shows a less sumptuous aspect. The street has fewer business premises being mostly occupied by hotels and refreshment rooms. Thomson's Restaurant boasts oysters and tripe suppers! The Bedford Hotel on the corner of St George's Place was rebuilt in 1886 as the Athenaeum, housing a restaurant, theatre, gymnasium and billiard room. Together with the former Liberal Club, it became the Royal Scottish Academy of Music and Drama from 1928–87. The Waverley Temperance Hotel became the Ivanhoe and more recently the Buchanan Hotel.

The greatest change in this part of Buchanan Street has been pedestrianisation and the intrusive maw of the **underground station**, reopened 11th April 1980.

SAUCHIEHALL STREET, GLASGOW LOOKING W. 11,305. G.W.W.

Sauchiehall Street is Glasgow's best known street perhaps due to the great variety of buildings along its length. At one end is the new International Concert Hall; at the other the Kelvin Hall and Art Galleries in Kelvingrove. Yet it is the now pedestrianised section where once the large department stores stood which is the most exciting. The earliest photograph was taken in the 1890s before Pettigrew and Stephen's dome and cupola joined Copeland and Lye's famous clock (cf. p. 134). The most attractive building on the north side had just been built for Cumming and Smith Ltd, house furnishers, which became the Savoy Cinema after 1913, and is now a shopping mall.

The Annan view taken in **1929** shows the south side the street completely rebuilt and occupied by bu nesses with familiar names, Watt Brothers on the site Garske's mantles and cloaks, Stobo, Thrift the tob conist, Birrells, Saxone and Barrett shoe shops and Jam Craig's tearooms. The latter had assumed the Cranst mantle after the demise of the Willow tearooms in 191 but Wendy's, opposite Trerons and Jean's further we also had their following.

In the 1990 photograph clock and cupola have gor making way for the **Sauchiehall Centre**, built in the '7 but recently revamped. Favourites such as Boots a Marks and Spencer continue to make the street a popu shopping precinct.

e view of **Sauchiehall Street at Charing Cross** has
.anged considerably in the last hundred years. The
.wly completed Charing Cross Mansions sit awk-
ardly against the backdrop of Albany Place, still the
ivate gardens of villas along the southern edge of
.rnethill.

Albany Chambers were added in 1899 completing
.e dramatic curve round to St George's Road. Even in
.s short time it seems the clock had ceased to function.
. spite of the presence of the Grand Hotel, the shops
. this quarter serve more domestic needs — a baker,
.ndry and branch post office.

With the coming of the motorway in 1970 the area
has changed dramatically. Only the Cameron Memorial
Fountain remains as a reminder of the 'grand' old days.
The restored **Charing Cross Mansions** are soon to be
overshadowed by Tay House. The developers,
TANAP, have included in their design a two-storey
restaurant on the 'bridge to nowhere' over the motorway. Unfortunately it will all face south west on to Bath
Street, turning its back on Charing Cross and last century's splendour.

The foundation stone of the new **University at Gilmorehill** was laid jointly by the Prince and Princess of Wales on 8th October 1868. The Prince and another member of the royal party, Prince John of Gluckstein, received the honorary degree of LL.D. — the first graduation ceremony on the hill!

The choice of an English architect, George Gilbert Scott, was not a popular one and was perhaps the reason for financial problems, leaving the building only two-thirds complete when it opened for Session 1870–71. Subsequent appeals provided the Bute and Randolph Halls (1884) and the **spire** in 1888. Appeals also saved the Lion and Unicorn Staircase from the Old College and the gateway and cornice which were later embodied in Pearce Lodge at the north east entrance to the University grounds.

GWW E4354

CLASGOW UNIVERSITY, FROM KELVINGROVE PARK. 10,447. G.W.W.

GWW C2018xa

During the **twentieth century** many **extensions** and
new premises have been added to the University site.
The memorial Chapel together with the Forehall completed the western side of the main building. It was
dedicated in 1929 to the seven hundred and fifty 'sons
of the University' who died in the Great War. The most
conspicuous additions — resembling something from
Gotham City — have been those on the north side of
University Avenue, most recently the new University
Library, Hunterian Museum and Art Gallery completed
in 1981. The University has always benefited from its
proximity to Kelvingrove Park, whose grassy slopes are
so tempting during the summer term!

Panorama from the University Tower

The **1905 view east** over the Kelvin to Park Circus shows the elegant terraces of Glasgow's finest west-end development, laid out by Charles Wilson c. 1860. The towers of Trinity College and Park Church look less imposing from this angle. The Prince of Wales Bridge in the foreground (1895) replaced a timber bridge painted to look like masonry, built in 1868 to accomodate the royal party when they laid the foundation stone of the University.

In July 1905 during Glasgow Fair when the factories were closed, T&R Annan took a famous series of **views from Glasgow University Tower**. Another series was taken in 1937. In July 1989 Stewart Shaw again photographed this panorama. Where change is dramatic, all three views are shown.

The **modern view looking east** shows a dramatic change in both vegetation and skyline. The cleaner atmosphere permits a view farther ben! In the northeast the motorway snakes past Cowcaddens and Townhead Church spire to the gasometers at Provan. The Royal Infirmary is visible behind the blocks of Townhead, but the City Chambers have disappeared behind the hotels and offices of the commercial centre.

1905, southeast over Kelvingrove Park to Anderston shows part of the old Kelvingrove Museum and the Saracen Fountain in the foreground. The Fountain was transferred to Alexandra Park when Kelvin Way was opened in 1915. In **1989** much of the Park is obscured by trees, but the Finnieston Crane and the Scottish Exhibition Centre help delineate the course of the Clyde.

STEWART SHAW

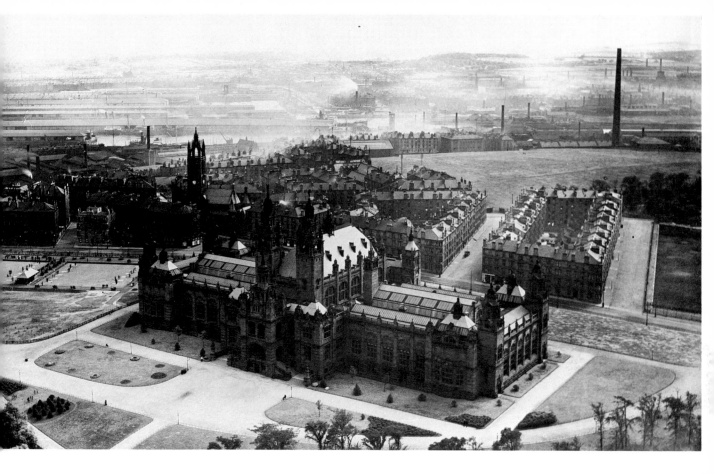

905, looks south over the Art Gallery and Museum
uilt with its front facing the Kelvin. The Clyde is still
hrouded in smog from many chimneys, including the

giant Refuse Dispatch Works near Pointhouse. The **1989 view** shows a redeveloped Yorkhill minus St Enoch's Free Church and the offending chimney.

STEWART SHAW

1905 looks west-southwest down the lower reaches of the Kelvin. In the foreground are the Materia Medica and Physiology Department being built in the first extension phase after the main University building was completed. Further down the hill is Partick Bridge, built for the Trustees of the Glasgow and Yoker Turnpike Roads. It superseded an earlier 18th century bridge a little upstream. Anderson's College of Medicine (1899) is on the edge of the Western Infirmary grounds on Dumbarton Road. Partick's famous mills on either side of the Kelvin are easily identified by their shapes. On the west bank, Scotstoun Mill stood on the site of the Waulk Mill begun in 1507 for the making of woollen cloth. The grain mills were built in 1877 and are still used by Rank Hovis Ltd to supply flour for their Duke Street bakery.

Across the Kelvin were the larger Regent Mills, also known as the Bunhouse Mill. They were owned by the SCWS producing their familiar 'Lofty Peak' flour. Downstream on the same side was the original mill of Partick, renamed Bishop Mill, founded by mediaeval monks in the 12th century. The lower reaches of the Kelvin were

taken over by the shipbuilding yards of A&J Inglis Pointhouse, and D&W Henderson of Meadowside. Ju visible on the other side of the Clyde is Govan Churc and the Fairfield Yard.

The **view in 1937** shows the Kelvin Hall (1926) built t replace earlier exhibition halls on the same site. It is no Glasgow's Museum of Transport and International Spor Arena. Yorkhill Hospital occupied the high ground the old lands of Overnewton. The large cranes and shec on the Clyde show shipbuilding still to the fore and th first Meadowside granary of thirteen bays and thirtee storeys (1913) is the structure further west.

In **1989** Meadowside has grown to a colossal thirty-fou bays, but sadly is closed and awaiting redevelopmen Cranes are concentrated round Kvaerner Govan Ltd a the Queen Mother Maternity Hospital now shares th Yorkhill site with the newer Royal Hospital for Sick Chi dren. The site of Regent Mills is a car park, the Bisho Mill is now flats, and Scotstoun Mill has been moder ised. Infirmary and University extensions are encroack ing on the park.

The **view looking west** shows how far the city has extended in the years between **1905** and **1989**. In the immediate foreground the sportsfield adjacent to the Botany Building on University Avenue has disappeared under the Zoology, Chemistry and Natural Philosophy departments. The west end of University Avenue has been realigned and modernised housing replaces much of the tenements of Hillhead and Hyndland. High-rise blocks in Broomhill, Scotstounhill and Knightswood can be seen in the far distance, with Gartnavel General Hospital in the middle distance.

STEWART SHAW

The **view looking northwest** to Dumgoyne and the Campsie Hills shows the extensive development of the intervening years. In **1905** the city stopped at the Maryhill gasworks with many greenfield sites between developments of west-end terraces and tenements. In **1989** in the foreground only University Gardens has sur-

vived amidst a forest of new development — the Boyd Orr building, the Queen Margaret Union, the Modern Languages building, the Adam Smith building and the new Library. Belmont Hillhead Church (1876) has been restored to its former glory but is overshadowed by the high-rise flats on the site of the old Maryhill Barracks.

STEWART SHAW

ANNAN OG306

Looking **north in 1905** two schools of note bound the photograph: Hillhead Public School in Cecil Street (1885), and Glasgow Academy, which moved from Elmbank Street in 1878. Hillhead House was demolished to make way for the Reading Room (1937), as was 6 Florentine Terrace in 1963, the gable-end house on the west side of Ann Street (renamed Southpark Avenue in 1922). This home of Charles and Margaret Mackintosh (1906 to 1914), was reconstructed within the new University Art Gallery and Museum. Wellington Church survives in **1989**, the congregation having moved in 18? from their earlier church in Wellington Street. Hillhead High School occupies the butterfly-shaped building (1931) and Ruchill Hospital tower (1900) can still be seen to the north.

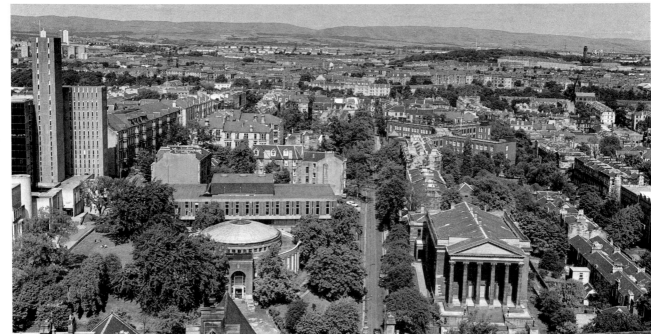

STEWART SHAW

...oking **north east in 1905** over Pearce Lodge and the ...lvin shows the many industrial lums of Port Dundas ...d St Rollox dwarfing the spires of Lansdowne Church ...d St Mary's Episcopal Church. In **1989** St Mary's spire ...shrouded in scaffolding but is now overshadowed by

tower blocks. In the middle distance much of the housing has been renovated or rebuilt and at the bottom of University Avenue the Rankine Building sits hard up against the Students Union (1931) which replaced the low terrace of shops including Stenhouse, the University bookshop.

ANNAN OG312

Unfortunately when T & R Annan took these panoramic views they could not have foreseen that one area of greatest change would fall at their overlap. Detail of the view over **Pearce Lodge (1905)** and **Park Circus (1937)** shows Cowcaddens, Port Dundas, St Rollox and Townhead before the motorway was pushed through in the period 1968-1975. Landmarks are the twin towers of t Corporation Electricity Station (so close together th look like one), Townsend's Stack on Crawford Street a (among others) the Tennant Stack in the distance. Bo of these were much reduced in height by 1937.

ANNAN OG317

landmark down the years is Townhead Parish Church (1866) which now stands high above the motorway alongside the neighbouring tower blocks. Other landmarks are the Provanmill gas works (1904) and the development in **1989** at Spiers Wharf, Port Dundas, where the old grain mills and a sugar refinery are being converted into 'yuppie' flats.

St George's Cross marked the city end of a turnpike road to Annie
land Toll authorised by Act of Parliament in 1836. The view loo
ing west (c. 1900) shows the spire of St Mary's Cathedral and La
downe Parish Church along Great Western Road with the Brit
Linen Bank dominating the corner of Clarendon Place. These bui
ings are still extant, but the road system has altered drastically
accommodate slip roads on the edge of the motorway. 'St Geor
and the Dragon' from the top of the old Cooperative building I
been preserved and was re-sited in 1988 on the pedestrianised p
of the Cross.

ANNAN OG243

e growth of villages south of the Clyde required the
ablishing of three tolls, all governing traffic over the
idges. One was on Rutherglen Loan, one on Main
eet south of Bedford Street, and one on Bridge Street
Nelson Street. Among the very few photographs of
t century Gorbals is this view on **Main Street looking**

north (1868). The area was then built up by the City
Improvement Trust, only to be swept away in the
rehabilitation of the 1960s. A new distinctive building is
the **Central Mosque**, completed in 1984, to serve the
Asian communities of the South Side.

STEWART SHAW

Anderston Cross

As navigation on the Clyde improved, the ports into the city increased to seven. The West Port on Trongate at the head of Stockwell Street was removed to **Anderston** and the toll with it. Anderston was a weaving village whose character changed in the nineteenth century due to its proximity to the river. Iron foundries, shipyards and engineshops, together with a hugely increased population meant a town of Victorian tenements. Anderston Cross Station opened in 1896 as part of the Glasgow Central railway. After World War II the area declined rapidly and has all but disappeared under the Kingston Bridge and the **motorway**.

STEWART SHAW

allowgate Toll

e original East Port of Glasgow stood on **Gallowgate**, old road to Edinburgh and England. By 1754 it was t 'a rickle o' stanes' and the toll was moved eastwards Witch Loan (Bellgrove Street). All the Glasgow tolls re abolished in 1878. The city's expansion necessi-

tated Improvement Trust tenements. Note the photographic studio high up on the roof to maximise daylight. Slum clearance under the GEAR Project (1976–87) has replaced the tenements with 'people-friendly' **housing schemes and gardens**.

The Clyde

The deep waters of the Firth of Clyde have always seen great ships in her harbours and fleets gathered in her shelter. After the American Civil War, Britain's first iron-clads, 'Black Prince' (built at Napier's Govan yard) and 'Warrior' were rendered obsolete by the invention of a superior armoured gun, which, mounted in a revolving turret, allowed it to fire in any direction irrespective of the position and course of the ship. The new iron-clad, **'Minotaur'**, photographed from the Esplanade, Greenock, was one of the longest single screw warships ever built, with fifty guns and a sail area the largest ever set in a warship.

Today Royal Navy vessels on the Clyde estuary are still a familiar sight — submarines en route to Faslane and frigates designed to destroy them! Yarrow Shipbuilders at Scotstoun received the 1990 Queen's Award for Technological Achievement for developing the **Type-23 Frigate**, the Royal Navy's most advanced surface warship. H.M.S. Lancaster, the latest Type-23, launched by her Majesty the Queen on 24th May 1990, is designed to operate with a complement of 150 men. She sets new standards of sonar efficiency and ship survivability, the latter as a result of the Navy's combat experience in the Falklands War.

Clutha

Cluthas or river steamers fir[st] sailed between Victoria Bridge a[nd] Whiteinch on 12th April 188[ ] Twelve were built by Thomas Sea[th] of Rutherglen for the Clyde Na[vi]gation Trust, and designed to car[ry] about 300 passengers at a penny [a] time. They called at jetties on eith[er] bank taking about forty-five minut[es] between their east-west des[ti]nations. By 1903 competition from t[he] trams and subway made the servi[ce] unprofitable and the last Clut[ha] made its final trip on 30th Novemb[er] of that year.

unnels

ossing the river has always pre-
nted problems especially to those
mmunities west of the harbour at
e Broomielaw. In earlier times
nnels and ferries were
nstructed, since bridges over the
vigation approach to the city
emed impossible. The first tunnels
der the Clyde were built by the
asgow Harbour Tunnel Company
Finnieston — three parallel
nnels, two for horsedrawn traffic
d one for pedestrians. The
tundas on each bank of the Clyde
ntained the stairs for pedestrians
d lifts for the vehicles. These
nnels closed to wheeled traffic in
43 and to pedestrians in 1980.
eir modern counterpart, **the
lyde Tunnel**, runs from Whiteinch
Linthouse. Completed in 1964 it
so has separated tunnels for cycle
d pedestrian traffic, one north and
e southbound.

STEWART SHAW

Ferries

Ferries over the Clyde have a much
longer history. The Clyde Navigation Trust introduced the double
chain steam ferry here at Govan in
1875, replacing smaller more vul-
nerable vessels. It is claimed this
could take eight horses and carts
plus 140 passengers or c. 500 passengers alone. In the 1890s there
were ferries at Erskine, Renfrew,
Whiteinch, Govan West, **Govan
Water Row**, Kelvinhaugh,
Stobcross, Clyde Street and York
Street. Of these only the Renfrew
Ferry remains, and the **site of the
Govan Ferry** is derelict.

F. LYALL

GWW's photograph of **morning on the Clyde** dates from around **1868**. It is a half of a stereo view of shipping west of the Broomielaw at a time when sail still out-numbered steam. The paddle steamer in the foreground is the PS Chevalier II, an iron twin funnelled vessel built for David Hutcheson & Co. by J & G Thomson of Clyde-bank. Hutcheson had three ships, 'Hero', 'Iona' and

'Chevalier' mainly employed on longer trips across t. lower firth and up the west coast. They were larger a. faster than the single funnelled paddle-steamers, a. above average in furnishings and appointments. H. cheson's ships were taken over by David MacBray. c. 1876 and were famous for their red and black funne. on the West Highland routes.

In 1990 the river vessels are for pleasure only. A refurbished Renfrew ferry at Clyde Street has become a
venue for music and cabaret. On a larger scale, the
former Stranraer-Larne car ferry 'Tuxedo Princess' is
moored at Anderston Quay as a 'floating palace of entertainment'. Beyond is the PS Waverley — the last ocean-
going paddle-steamer in the world (cf. p. 113). The river
is now spanned by the **Kingston Bridge** — ten lanes of
urban motorway sixty feet above the navigation channel,
completed in 1970, but already showing need for repair
due to the volume of traffic it carries. The South Rotunda
of the old Harbour Tunnel is in use as an exhibition
centre. In 1990 it housed the Dome of Discovery, allowing hands-on participation in science and technology
exhibits.

GWW E3334

GWW's photo shows **Telford's Broomielaw Bridge** (1833–5) before the view was obscured by the Caledonian Railway Bridge of 1876–7. The latter was subsequently widened from four to thirteen tracks in 1904 to accommodate the increase in rail traffic to and from Central Station. The Merchants' Steeple and the spire of Gorbals Parish Church (before it was damaged by lightning) can be seen in Annan's pre-1925 view of the **Clyde from the Sailor's Home**.

om 1768, the process of creating and maintaining a
vigable channel was the responsibility of the Clyde
avigation Trust (housed under the Dome on the north
nk of the river) and a constraint on Bridge Trustees.
e **King George V Bridge** seen here in construction

and completed (1925) needed an arch of 18½ feet above
high water to accommodate puffers and dredgers. Burns
and Laird Line operated their boats to Belfast from the
quay in the foreground.

Jamaica Bridge

Wilson's early view (c. 1868) shows **Telford's Bridge** was a steep climb for horsedrawn traffic. It proved too narrow for the age of trams, its foundations too shallow and its arches too inconvenient for shipping. The Annan photograph of 1894 shows an accommodation bridge upstream prior to Jamaica Bridge being rebuilt. Paisley's store now occupies the site of Thomson, the clothier, and Townsend's stack has been reduced in size. Below St Enoch's Church and the Station Hotel are the sheds of Customhouse Quay. The **1910 view** shows the alterations completed and trams and lights electrified.

Today the trams and traffic islands have gone, traffic is now one-way, south-bound, and the view to the north side of the river has changed competely. Clyde Hall (Strathclyde University) rises dramatically from the corner of Jamaica and Clyde Streets and the glass of the St Enoch Centre replaces the Hotel and Station.

The Suspension Bridge

THE CLYDE, ABOVE THE BROOMIELAW, GLASGOW. 1340. GWW.

The **Suspension Bridge** opposite South Portland Street was opened on 18th May 1853 by the Lord Provost who walked from the south side and back again accompanied by a band playing 'The Garb of Old Gaul'! The bridge was erected by the Gorbals Trustees to replace a wooden accommodation bridge built when the first Broomielaw Bridge was itself being rebuilt by Thomas Telford. It had proved so useful that it had survived until it became unsafe in 1846. In the background is the Merchant's Steeple and **St Andrew's Roman Catholic Cathedral**. Boats on the river include the small PS 'Clyde', built 1861, and a mud punt or dredger. Two hundred and fifty years ago the river was only eighteen inches at low tide, with many shoals and islands. John Smeaton was commissioned to survey the river for possible bridge sites, while John Golbourne of Chester was engaged to find means to deepen the channel of the river to seven feet (even at neap tides) from Dumbrec Ford near Dumbarton to the Broomielaw. This h accomplished by building a series of one hundred an seventeen jetties from the banks, causing the river scour a deep channel for itself. Since then dredger have continued to maintain the channel. The sludge wa emptied into hopper barges which took it to the firth unload in deep water.

A major problem of last century was the untreated sewage which found its way into the river from the mar Lanarkshire communities upstream, as well as from Glasgow itself. The river stank! When a system of intercepting sewers was laid at the turn of the century pur fication works were built at Dalmuir and Shieldhall. No the river has recovered and fish are to be had in i waters once more, as the **cormorant on the Clyde** ca testify.

STEWART SHAW

The Victoria and Albert Bridges

This **aerial view of the Clyde** looking downstream from Glasgow Green shows Glasgow in the **mid-1970s** during a period of great upheaval. Vast tracts on either side of the river have been cleared and await redevelopment. In the distance the Finnieston Crane and Queen's Dock can be identified beyond the Kingston Bridge. Coming upstream, the next river crossings are the three bridges at Broomielaw. A very thin Suspension Bridge is next and then the SV 'Carrick' moored on the north bank next the Victoria Bridge. This last is the oldest Clyde bridge in the city, built in 1851–4 on the site of the origina mediaeval Glasgow Bridge at the foot of Stockwell Stre and Bridgegate. Upstream from it is the City Unic Railway Bridge of 1899. It carried four lines of track from the south, mainly to the now demolished St Enoch Station The bridge nearest the camera is the Albert Bridge. was opened in 1871 and is the fifth bridge to be built or near the end of Saltmarket since 1795. The Justiciar Court House and Jail were built in 1814 (and rebuilt 1913) replacing the Tolbooth as court and jail.

The **view looking downstream in 1990** is a much happier one. The gap sites have been filled — the Scottish Exhibition Centre on Queen's Dock, the Sheriff Court and the Central Mosque now occupy sites at Gorbals Cross and the St Enoch Centre is where the station and hotel used to be. The edge of the river has now been landscaped with the Clyde Walkway and the city has the look of many a European capital!

Shipbuilding

1829 when the Glasgow Association of Underwriters
and Brokers instituted a register of shipping, it was found
that Glasgow with eighty-nine vessels was the fifth port
in Scotland, behind Aberdeen (374), Greenock (338),
Leith (213) and Port Glasgow (118). But Henry Bell's
'Comet', launched eight years earlier was to change the
course of shipbuilding in Glasgow's favour. Yards on
the lower Clyde had built up a skill in wooden shipbuilding — Scotts of Greenock, J & C Wood of Port
Glasgow and W. Denny of Dumbarton. Numerous
smaller yards survived because the amount of fixed
capital involved was not great, thus encouraging many
shipbuilders to set up on their own account. Most were
short-lived, especially as the trend towards iron ships
grew. One such company was Scott & Linton on the
Leven which went bankrupt during the building of the
'Cutty Sark' (1869). She was a sailing vessel built to carry
passengers and cargo (usually tea) at speed over vast
distances. Because tea quickly lost its flavour in the hold
of a ship, annual prizes were offered by London merchants for the speediest delivery of the first crop of the
season. There was much competition in the famous China

tea clipper races from Foo Chow to London, with
extravagant claims made by the ship's captains. 'Cutty
Sark' set a record in her time for one day's travel of 363
miles, but this was soon eclipsed by the 380 miles run
by 'Thermopylae' built by Walter Hood in Aberdeen for
the White Star Line. **'Cutty Sark'** was photographed
while acting as a coal tender in Lisbon c. 1920, and probably owes her enormous reputation to her preservation
at Greenwich, as one of the only two clippers in the
world to have survived. The other is the **SV 'Carrick'**
built in Sunderland in 1864 as the 'City of Adelaide'
which carried 1500 tons of cargo plus passengers to and
from Australia. She holds the record for a sailing ship
passage from London to Adelaide of sixty-five days. The
Royal Naval Volunteer Reserve has owned the 'Carrick'
since 1947 and ran her as a floating club downstream
from Victoria Bridge. In 1990 she was sold for the nominal
sum of £1 to the Clyde Ship Trust, established to build a
£20m heritage centre in Glasgow. The 'Carrick' will be
restored to her former glory and exhibited with three
Clyde-built vessels the Trust hopes to acquire.

Although Henry Bell is celebrated as the father of shipbuilding on the Clyde, his role was that of entrepreneur rather than inventor. He married the skill of J & C Wood, who built the Comet's hull, with that of James Robertson and David Napier, who designed and built its engine and boiler. It was **Robert Napier**, David's cousin, who made the Clyde's reputation for shipbuilding. He opened his first shipyard at Govan in 1841. He also secured Parkhead Forge and the Lancefield Works from David Napier to control the quantity and quality of his supplies for engines and hulls. Though iron ships were more expensive to build than wooden ones, running costs were as much as twenty-five per cent less, and therefore attractive to passenger fleet owners. Lloyds and the Admiralty soon followed the trend.

Robert Napier built the first iron ship for Cunard, the **PS 'Persia'**, photographed by Thomas Annan on the stocks at Govan in 1855. 'Persia' was then the largest vessel in the world, with a speed of thirteen knots. Napier had earlier helped finance Samuel Cunard's North American Royal Mail Steam Navigation Company, and by constantly upgrading designs and offerin improvements, he won the majority of Cunard contrac for twenty years. In 1862 he built the 'Black Prince' f the Navy, Britain's second iron-clad warship, and tł most famous of the thirty ships he built for the Nav between 1843 and 1876.

Moss and Hume describe Napier's firm as 'the kin-rgarten of Clyde Shipbuilders'. The majority of com-ting yards were set up by former employees, notably G Thomson (which became John Brown Shipbuilding d Engineering Co. Ltd.) and Randolph and Elder hich became Fairfield Shipbuilding and Engineering . Ltd.). These two were to take over from Napier's as ders in their field. Elder's also poached the skills of pier's shipyard manager William Pearce, who was imately responsible for the success of the new yard Fairfield. Under his management the yard acquired ge stakes in shipping companies in part-payment for ps (108 as compared to 44 built by J & G Thomson 30–88). Pearce also obtained a significant number of lmiralty contracts which continued after his death der the yard's new director, Sir William Arrol. The

photograph shows the **blading of turbine rotors c. 1914**.

After World War I all the yards on the Clyde experi-enced depression, and Fairfield's changed hands, bought first by the Northumberland Shipbuilding Group, and in 1933 by the Lithgow Group. Re-armament and the Second World War postponed closure until 1965 when the Geddes Inquiry into Shipbuilding rec-ommended the amalgamation of the Upper Clyde yards of John Brown, Fairfield, Connell, Stephen and Yarrow into UCS Ltd. The hope of building standard cargo-ships on a production-line basis was never realised and the company was liquidated in 1972, resulting in the famous take-over by workers and shopstewards. Government bowed to pressure and with subsidies the yard survived first as Govan Shipbuilders, and now as Kvaerner Govan Ltd., employing 1500.

The brothers James and George Thomson had both worked for Robert Napier, one as foreman at Lancefield, the other as leading smith, finisher and turner. They opened their own ship-yard at Govan, building one hundred and ten vessels between 1851 and 1872, including their first Blue Riband holder, the 'Russia', for Cunard. With the prospect of tendering for larger ships they moved downstream to opposite the mouth of the Cart at Clydebank. The trend towards building larger vessels continued — the 'America', 'City of New York' and 'City of Paris' were fitted with a luxury and magnificence unequalled at the time. But the practice of building loss-leaders to encourage custom, (so successful in Napier's yard), spelled disaster for large complex ships of this type. The firm was taken over in

1899 by John Brown & Co. of Sheffield, who re-equipp the yard for the building of a wider range of vesse As well as joining the Coventry Syndicate, John Brov acquired a majority shareholding in Harland and Wc of Belfast, securing control of the British shipbuildi capacity for large passenger liners. But after the Fi World War even orders for liners dried up, and t largest of them all, ship no. 534, was left on the stoc when work stopped on 12th December 1931. It to pressure from David Kirkwood, MP, to get a loan for t work to proceed. The **'Queen Mary'** was launched 26th September 1934 and, along with her sister sh 'Queen Elizabeth' did valiant service as a troop-sh during the War. She is now preserved as a floating ho in Long Beach, California.

OSCAR MARZAROLI

...lkhead 231, photographed in 1967, was to become the ...ost prestigious British ship of the post-war era, the ...E II'. The smallest of the three Queens, she was never-...eless 963 feet long, and was designed to carry over ...00 passengers at a cruising speed of 32.5 knots. She ...as launched in September 1967, the same month that ...hn Brown's became part of the Upper Clyde Ship-...ilders in terms of the recommendation of the Geddes ...eport of 1966. Her trials were not auspicious — major ...oblems with oil seepage and turbine damage caused ...nard to refuse payment of the final £1.5m, this giving

UCS its first liquidity crisis.

QE II finally sailed from Southampton on her maiden voyage to New York in May 1969. As well as regular trans-Atlantic crossings April to December, she does a winter round-the-world cruise as part of her annual schedule. In 1982 she sailed for the Falklands as a troop-ship, following in the tradition of the earlier Queens. A major refit in a German yard in 1986–7 caused much indignation on Clyde-side, but all seemed forgotten when she visited the Clyde on 25 July 1990 as part of the 1990 celebrations.

Construction

In the second half of the 19th centu
construction industry produced in Gla
a central business district which was s
to none. Prosperity produced privat
commercial buildings of such magnifi
that they were featured extensively in
photographer's catalogue. Espe
apparent in the old photographs ar
amazing sculptured figures and car
which most architects of the day used t
orate and enhance their masterp
Between 1840 and 1890 most were the
of one family business, the Mossma
William, John and George, monun
sculptors in Mason Street near the Cath
John Mossman was the best known
family and was responsible for many
statues in the city — David Living
James Lumsden and Norman MacLe
Cathedral Square and Thomas Campbe
Sir Robert Peel in George Square.
larger scale were the figures incorpo
in the buildings of the new City Cham
the Athenaeum, the Clyde Navigation
and St Andrew's Halls. The remar
photo of **J & G Mossman's yard** shows
of these figures in preparation c. 1875,
ibly the caryatids for St Andrew's
James Sellar's masterpiece.

Andrew's Halls were gutted by fire in 1962 and for
ars Glasgow lacked a suitable concert venue in spite
its being home to most of Scotland's classical com-
nies — the Scottish National Orchestra, Scottish Opera
and Scottish Ballet and the BBC Scottish Symphony
Orchestra, The new **Royal Concert Hall** designed by
Sir Leslie Martin is a fitting legacy of Glasgow's Year of
Culture celebrations in 1990.

FORTH BRIDGE, FROM SOUTH. 6971. G.W.W.
HEIGHT 369. Ft.   LENGTH-(INCLUDING VIADUCT)- 8096. Ft.   SPANS - 1710. Ft. EACH.

Structural engineering in Glasgow grew out of iron founding as builders and engineers experimented with its possible implications. Iron-framed buildings, mostly mills and warehouses, appeared in the early 1800s and cast-iron bridges for road and rail crossings were built even as late as 1890, eg. the Great Western Road bridge over the Kelvin. **William Arrol** was Glasgow's foremost bridge builder. The firm's Caledonian Railway Bridge (1876–78) was the construction which established the company. They were contractors for the second Tay Bridge (1882–87), made in sections at Dalmarnock, and for an overlapping period a major contractor for the

Forth Railway Bridge (1883–90). A yard at the Sou Queensferry end of the bridge made the steel on site was William Arrol's own thoroughness and ingenu which solved many problems. He even had replicas the central span built on an estate in Ross-shire to test structural strength. He was knighted on the completi of the Bridge in 1890. His firm went on to build Tow Bridge in London (1893), Glasgow's Jamaica Brid (1895–99), the North Bridge, Edinburgh (1895–99) a in this century the Forth Road Bridge and the Humb Bridge. The firm finally ceased operations on 3 October 1986.

In recent times it is the ring road, proposed in 1946 by Robert Bruce, Glasgow City Engineer, which has had the greatest impact on the face of the city and its subsequent fortune. The Highways Plan of 1965 modified the original intention but created the motorway which scythes the city in two. Connecting the north and south sections of road is the Kingston Bridge, completed in 1970. Oscar Marzaroli's photograph of the **approach to the Kingston bridge during construction (1968)** emphasises the change in structural engineering from Arrol's time. The tall columns, reminiscent of some cathedral, were to support triple-cell, pre-stressed concrete box girders cast in situ, carrying two parallel highways each with five lanes of traffic. In 1990 cracks appeared which necessitated repairs and underlined the urgency for another motorway bridge to be built across the Clyde.

Engineerin

Engineering in the west of Scotland has
origins in the technical expertise built up
service the cotton industry. When iron a
steel replaced wood, the proximity of iron a
coal encouraged millwrights to turn their sk
to heavier industries such as mining and ste
engineering. For a time the greatest dema
for engines was for the manufacture of sug
machinery for export, reflecting the trad
links between the Glasgow sugar barons a
the West Indies. But the American Civil W
and the Crimean War stimulated new effo
Robert Napier started as a millwright a
engine-builder and, with his cousin's ing
uity, pioneered marine engineering on
Clyde. They worked forges at Lancefield, Ca
lachie and **Parkhead**. The last was managed
Napier's son-in-law William Rigby, who to
on William Beardmore as a partner in 18
Beardmore's son, also William, assumed co
plete control in 1886.

ung William Beardmore had been educated at Ander-
's College and the School of Mines in London. He
anded the business, bought out the parent company,
pier & Son in 1900, and started a new shipyard at
muir. New plant worth £250,000 was built at
khead, including a 12,000 ton hydraulic press and
n tempering shop. The company also took over faces for aero-engines and motor cars, but by 1927 the
n's losses were as spectacular as had been its pre-
r success. The company was restructured and Beard-
re, now Lord Invernairn, was forced to retire. Park-
d survived the Second World War supplying armour
te and small arms, and was nationalised in 1949. The
lliam Beardmore Company finally ceased trading in
'5. A **silence** descended on Parkhead and the sur-
nding district which it had not known for a hundred
l fifty years. The noise of the hammers and the roar
en the furnace opened had been woven into the fibre
east-end folk and the hush was symptomatic of death.
e GEAR (Glasgow Eastern Area Renewal) Project was
up in 1976 to encourage a phoenix to rise from the
es. In Parkhead some success is visible in the shape
the new shopping centre opened in October 1988.
propriately named **The Forge**, it has seventy-five
aller units, two larger ones, a multi-screen cinema
d parking for 2000 cars.

STEWART SHAW

F. LYALL

89

Locomotive building in the Glasgow area developed because of the region's natural resources of coal and iron, and the existence of expertise in forging and engineering. As with shipbuilding, one man's company was the kindergarten from which the other firms developed. Walter Neilson started a partnership (c. 1836) making sugar machinery and land and marine engines. In 1842 his firm built the winding engine at the top of the Cowlairs incline to ensure a means of bringing trains safely up and down to Queen Street Station. Soon he specialised in locomotive building and in 1860 moved from Finnieston to his new **Hyde Park Works** in Springburn with a link to the Edinburgh and Glasgow railway. His manager was then Henry Dubs (possibly the top-hatted figure in Annan's photograph). In 1865 Dubs left to set up his own works south of the Clyde at Polmadie and James Reid succeeded him at Hyde Park. He in turn managed to take over the Hyde Park Works in 1876 and Walter Neilson was obliged to set up new works on the opposite side of Springburn Station. By then he was an old man, and the business at the new Clyde Locomotive Works did not prosper. They were taken over by Sharp Stewart & Co. of Manchester, and renamed the Atlas Works.

Alongside the private locomotive builders were railway companies. The Edinburgh and Glasg[ow] Railway Company set up workshops west of its main l[ine] at **Cowlairs** in 1842. When it became the North Brit[ish] Railway Co. in 1865, production of the famous gre[en] liveried locomotives began in earnest. One of their m[ost] famous engines was the 'Diver', so called after it w[ent] down with the Tay Bridge on 27 December 1879. T[he] engine was recovered, refurbished at Cowlairs, and [gave] another thirty years' service! Between 1842 and 1924 [the] company built c. 850 locos, but when it became the LN[ER] the works became solely a repair shop. After nation[al]isation it continued to repair steam locomotives u[ntil] 1968 when British Rail abandoned steam and Cowla[irs] was closed. Modern **Intercity trains** are now all s[er]viced in England. The Caledonian Railway Compan[y] works at St Rollox followed a similar pattern. From 1[8__] to 1923 they built c. 1000 locomotives, among then[m] famous Dunalastairs, called after the then chairm[an] James Bunten of Dunalastair. When the company beca[me] part of the LMS in 1923 the works concentrated [on] repairs. British Rail closed St Rollox in 1986 and pl[ans] for housing, shops, a business park and leisure facilit[ies] are being promoted by the S.D.A.

91

GAG&M-PP

S&T

S&T

the 1901 International Exhibition the **Machinery Hall** as full of gleaming engines from each of the main Scottish companies. Visitors surveyed the scene from galleries that went the entire length of the Hall (500 ft). he stand nearest the camera belong to Dubs & Co.'s asgow Locomotive Works.

Up to 1903 the three Glasgow rivals had built 16,000 comotives of which only 2000 were for the home arket. In 1903 they amalgamated to form the North itish Locomotive Company, the largest locomotive mpany outside America and known locally as 'The ombine'! It was a common sight to see **locomotives aving Hyde Park** on the stately journey to the docks. ere the giant **Finnieston crane** loaded them like toys r any one of sixty different countries. The Atlas and de Park Works had over 8000 employees involving ost families in Springburn.

During World War I tanks, mines and shells were also ade, but, as with shipbuilding, the two World Wars ly postponed the company's eventual demise. It failed make the transition from steam to diesel and closed 1962. Only **George Wylie's straw locomotive** made r Mayfest 1987 has hung from the crane since then.

STEWART SHAW

93

The aim of the **1888 International Exhibition** was to promote Science and Art and to stimulate commercial enterprise. It was also hoped to fund a new Art Gallery and Museum and a School of Art from the profits. The main pavilion in Kelvingrove Park had an oriental look — indeed it was nicknamed 'Baghdad on the Kelvin'. The Exhibition was opened by the Prince of Wales in May and was visited by Queen Victoria in August when she also 'opened' the City Chambers.

In **1901** another Exhibition was held to inaugurate the new Art Gallery and Museum. A magnificent temporary Industrial Hall was sited next to the new Gallery. But the death of the Queen earlier in 1901 cast the **opening ceremony** into half-mourning with Princess Louise, the new King's daughter, officiating.

The **Empire Exhibition in 1938** was an attempt to revive the spirit of industrial Scotland after the Depression years. It was also an expression of hope and peace in a world on the verge of another war. The location at Bellahouston Park allowed a larger exhibition than could have been mounted in the confined space of Kelvingrove Park. The abiding memory of this event was Tait's Tower (named after the Exhibition's designer) from which could be seen much of Glasgow, including the new 'Queen' on the stocks at John Brown's.

GDC

1988 the Glasgow Garden Festival signified resurgence from another period of economic depression. The site at Prince's Dock was an epitome of the city's decline now earmarked for revival. The District Council maximised the catalysing effect of the Festival for the whole city with an emphasis on projects that made Glasgow 'look and feel good'.

Memorable in the Eye and Ear Garden was this globe of the living world — *Alternanthera* for the land masses and *Sagina* for the sea, planted in peat on a glass-fibre mould and ingeniously watered by the 'arm' as the globe revolved on its axis. Rose-coloured spectacles helped folk to see the world differently!

Manufacturing

When the American War of Independen interrupted tobacco supplies to Scotland, me chants looked for other raw materials to their ships. Among sugar, rum and cotton it w the last which ushered in a new phase of t Industrial Revolution in the west of Scotland transformed a domestic textile industry into urban environment of mills and factories, b achfields and printworks. Yet another Ame ican War disrupted supplies forcing a seve contraction in the industry, but as late as 18 the 48,500 textile workers vastly outnumber the 4,500 shipbuilding and engineerir workers in Glasgow and Govan. The rol were reversed by 1900 but specialists li Templeton's, the carpet manufacturers, su vived into the 20th Century on the back of shi building's many large orders for passeng liners (eg. ten miles of carpeting were require for the Queen Mary!). Many women we employed in the lighter, more tedious jobs the industry such as **bobbin winding** or t **weaving of chenille**, used in the manufactu of Axminster carpets.

GR

G&G&M·PP

96

GAG&M-PP

As well as satisfying local demand, **cabinet-makers** and furniture manufacturers also benefited from the fitting-out of luxury ships and there were close links with the textile manufacturers for their range of upholstery supplied.

Today local furniture manufacturers are specialists still aiming to please the luxury end of the market. One such, **Mackintosh and Company**, are creating quality reproductions of furniture designed by C. R. Mackintosh and his contemporaries.

STEWART SHAW

Robert F. Barr, son of a soft drinks manufacturer in Falkirk, set up on his own account at Parkhead in 1887. 'Old Scotch' Ginger Beer, lemonade and soda water were early favourites, followed by later imaginatively named products such as iron brew, sarsaparilla and American Cream Soda.

A. G. Barr, for whom the present company is named, was the first in Glasgow to introduce bottles with re-sealable screw stoppers. This was a boon to consumers as well as to employees, of whom not a few had lost an eye as a result of explosions when working the early bottling machine. By **1930** a new **semi-automated bottling line** had been installed allowing 53 bottles to be filled per minute. By comparison the **new automated line** (opposite) fills 400 bottles per minute.

Scotland's other national 'drink'

The firm has always had sparkling advertising to match their products. In the 1920s a large sign 'ASK FOR BARR'S MINERAL WATERS' matched that of Wilson's Colosseum in Jamaica Street. In the 1930s a weekly cartoon featuring the adventures of Ba-Bru and Sandy captured the imagination of Bulletin readers. The **Ba-Bru sign above Central Station** (opposite) appeared about 1947. After World War II, when utility labelling ended and companies were once more allowed to advertise their products, Barr took the decision to change their most famous drink to 'Irn-Bru'. This was in part to continue the pre-war association with Ba-Bru, but more in anticipation of new labelling regulations where accuracy of description was to be enforced. In fact legislation was delayed till 1964 and included a 'grandfather rule' to permit products of long-standing to continue with their original name. In 1970 the cartoon gave way to commercials of a different kind on television. 'Made in Scotland from girders' and 'Your Other National Drink' still promote Irn-Bru. The sign was changed in 1983 and **Graham Barr**, the son of the chairman helped with the publicity. In 1987 the firm took over the St Clement's range, to become the UK's largest soft drink manufacturers with a turnover of around £88 million and a staff of 1500.

(GH) A.G. BARR PLC

STEWART SHAW

Commerce and Trade

The tradition of street vendors and corner shops is one which happily has not vanished from the Glasgow scene, though the style has altered considerably. **Cuddy Tam** was one of Springburn's local heroes who sold rhubarb and other vegetables from a donkey cart at the turn of the century. He is photographed in front of William Graham's studio at 21 Vulcan Street. In 1956 the **flower-seller in Union Street** preferred her customers to come to her, but all are met with a cheery grin. Now street vendors are mostly to be found in the pedestrian precincts of Buchanan Street, Argyle Street, and Sauchiehall Street.

The **London and Glasgow Tea Company** at the corner of Springburn Road and Kay Street c. 1907 was a very superior establishment with all kinds of delicacies in the window, from Irish eggs and Belfast bacon to American hams and Scotch salmon. By comparison **Govanhill's 5 star grocer** prefers to use his window space for advertisements emphasising everything on special offer!

STEWART SHAW

'Barra Patter'

Glasgow retailers have always had style, with a rich contrast between east and west end. The textile industry was concentrated in the Calton with a rag-trade and second-hand clothes market second to none. Poverty forced many Calton folk to earn their living as street hawkers, giving rise to Paddy's Market and the Barrows. Peter Fyfe (1854–1940) was a Chief Sanitary Inspector so burdened by the grinding conditions in the east end that he made a photographic record in the years before the First World War. Whether photographing bare-foot children or hawkers with their **barrows in Moncur Street**, he captured the spirit of the east end, which was also the hall-mark of Oscar Marzaroli's photographs of fifty years later.

STEWART SHAW

The Barras as we know it today was established b Maggie and James McIver in the early 1920s. They ha earlier been in the business of renting out barrows 1s 6d per week to stallholders in and around Gallowga When a number of tenements were demolished, t McIvers bought the ground for a permanent market sit built stalls and eventually roofed it over in 1928. The also opened the famous Barrowland Ballroom, whe many local girls (including Lena Martell and Lulu) mac their names as singers and visitors such as Joe Loss a Henry Hall experienced an east-end baptism! The Barr have been the inspiration of many songs and stories such as Matt McGinn (1928–77) and Billy Connolly. recounts his fascination with Barra patter and one of masters, who threw pens at his audience to get the attention —
'A green yin fer a Fenian
An orange wan fer an Orange man!'

'Glasgow Style'

By contrast, retailers in Glasgow's (then) west end developed a wholly different strategy. Drapers' warehouses were transformed into department stores, some with fanciful names such as Anderson's Polytechnic and Wilson's Colosseum. In Buchanan Street the first Hugh Fraser had to compete with Wylie and Lochhead's innovations such as a steam lift and spacious galleries. These were for promenading through and lingering in, encouraging people to touch and try the goods which were temptingly displayed. The war of winning customers brought ever brighter decor and sumptuous surroundings. Tea rooms were introduced to tempt ladies to dally with friends and **fashion shows** were arranged to draw attention to the latest vogue. Gradually one firm came to dominate the department stores of Glasgow, largely because of the energies of the third Hugh Fraser, who became chairman of House of Fraser in 1941. Wylie Hills, Arnott Simpson's, Pettigrew and Stephen and arch-rivals Wylie and Lochhead came under the Fraser banner as well as other famous Scots and English stores, the jewel in the crown being Harrod's in Knightsbridge.

In the 1980s shopping patterns changed and now many retailers are opting for the American shopping mall unit, where even the street is indoors. The Forge, **St Enoch Centre** and the new Buchanan Centre (1993) offer Glaswegians the combination of department stores and small specialist shops together under the same roof.

STEWART SHAW

OSCAR MARZAROLI

e work of women in the 19th century was generally
sregarded by photographers, but Peter Fyfe's Col-
ction included them in his survey of the Calton.
ashing day in this back court (opposite) was obviously
good time for a gossip and exchange of news. Notice
e sink at the top of the stairs beside the window. It was
own in Ulster and in Glasgow as the 'jaw-box', 'jaw'
eaning to 'pour'. Over the years the conversations
ld over this sink unit came to use the same word. A
od 'jaw' was always to be had in the steamies of the
th century.

'Steamies' evolved from the traditional wash-houses
built round the Green and in other areas rebuilt by the
City Improvement Trust. They also included Public Baths
to encourage personal hygiene. Tenement houses had
back-court drying greens often with a communal wash-
house. This was a continual source of frustration and
disagreement, as washing had to be done by rota in
spite of weather, and woe betide anyone who lost the
wash-house key! The washing was strung up usually
beside the ashpits, and as late as 1977 women preferred
to bring washing to the clothes poles on the Green.

In the Street

Glasgow children have always excelled at **street games**, especially in the poorer areas where toys were a luxury 'to be kept on the mantle and played with on Sunday.' Ball games, peeries, hoops and beds were accompanied by traditional rhymes with contemporary verses. Nevertheless chores had to be done, but, when everyone joined in, the kindling sticks were split that much faster. Who nowadays would permit children of this age near a cleaver like the one held by the girl in the centre of the picture?

In the **Gorbals in the 1960s** things hadn't changed very much. Though the children are better clad, the presence of a removal van gave opportunity for some high jinks, but once the flitting was complete it would be back to balls and peevors once more.

SRA

FOUNTAIN UNIVERSITY WESTENDPARK GLASGOW 1342 G.W.W.

GWW E1718

Water Games

Water games varied depending on your social status. These lads photographed near the effluent-filled Molendinar weren't worried about the health hazards — it was an exciting place to play. Following the water-cart held similar attractions especially on a hot summer's day in 1916. For children in Kelvingrove Park in 1870 the Stewart Fountain was fascinating. In 1990 just looking is too tame, and while the water jets are stopped children have a paddle and a climb.

GLASGOW HERALD

STEWART SHAW

109

e famous football clubs of Glasgow both trace their gins to enthusiasts who met on Glasgow Green. leed as early as 1574 six 'futt balls' per annum were d for out of the civic purse for the use of folk playing the Green. **Rangers** was founded in 1873 by a number lads who, after an evening's rowing, used to play a me of football on Fleshers' Haugh. They moved to a vate field off Great Western Road in 1885, to the first ox Park via Kinning Park in 1887 and to their present und in 1899. Moses McNeil, extreme right in the oto of the 1876–7 team, was captain and the first Ranr's player to play for Scotland. Rangers joined the .A. in 1874, winning the Cup for the first time in 1894. Celtic Football Club was founded with a more philhropic end in mind. It was hoped to raise funds for needy children in the missions of St Mary's, Sacred art and St Michael's, Bridgeton. The first Celtic Park s the site now occupied by A. G. Barr, their first game

20th May 1888 — they won 5–2 and won the Scottish Cup three years later. They moved to their present home in 1892 and in 1967 were the first British Club to win the European Cup.

Much is made of the rivalry between these two teams, divided by religious and ethnic differences. Rangers are viewed as staunchly Protestant Lowland Scots; Celtic as Roman Catholic of Irish and Gaelic origins. The truth is somewhere in between — Celtic have fielded Protestant players since the 1920s and won the European Cup under a Protestant manager, Jock Stein. Rangers were slower to grasp the nettle, but in 1989 signed **Maurice Johnston**, a former Celtic player and son of a Protestant father and Catholic mother. The religious bigotry associated with the two clubs will take a long time to die, but every small step counts. They are the Yang and Yin of Glasgow's football scene and need one another to survive.

111

Doon the Watter

Before the age of the train, Clyde paddle steamers were the only reliable means of transporting cargo and passengers down the Clyde, in the Firth and to the Western Isles. In many places the existence of a pier encouraged property development and population increase. From being all-year round river buses, soon the new habit of going 'doon the watter' meant a rapid increase in traffic at weekends and in summer. Resorts expanded to cope with demands and to attract trade, shipowners vied with one another in the amenities and the speed of their vessels. Officially racing was frowned upon, but many captains flouted the rules, openly encouraged by their passengers, who viewed it as part of their day's entertainment.

GWW's photo **'Embarking at the Broomielaw'** captures some of this excitement. The PS 'Chancellor' with the double white striped funnel started service c. 18 on the run to Arrochar under command of Capt: Neilson. She called at Greenock, Dunoon, Hunte Quay, Blairmore and Craigendoran. The paddlesteam with 'Royal Mail' on the paddle box was an older st flush-decked steamer called the 'Vivid'. She was b by Barclay Curle & Co. in 1844 but sustained terri damage when she ran into floating timber which h broken loose from a pound at Greenock during a stor She was refitted and sold to Captain Buchanan for wo mainly among the upper Clyde piers.

THE BEN MORE LEAVING THE BROOMIELAW, GLASGOW. 5027 G.W.W.

ose who liked sailing in comfort had many paddle-
amers to choose from. The **'Ben More'** seen leaving
omielaw for Kilmun was built in 1876 by Thomas Seath
Co. of Rutherglen (the 'clutha' manufacturers). She
ed under the Buchanan flag for many years, mostly
the Rothesay run.

The **PS 'Waverley'** is the last of her kind still taking
Glaswegians on pleasure trips. Built in 1947 by A. & J.
Inglis of Pointhouse she replaced the third steamer of
the same name which was sunk at Dunkirk while requi-
sitioned for naval duties in 1940.

113

The Fair

In 1890 an Act of Parliament permitted the railway companies to build and operate their own steamers. By operating time-tables to suit their large, faster vessels they were able to halve the travelling time to resorts. Edwardian Glaswegians obviously approved of this change as the crowds in the **Central Station on Fair Saturday** show.

Fair Saturday in the '90s shows a modernised Central Station and fewer people. Destinations on the board are still the places traditionally served by the Caledonian Railway — Ardrossan, West Kilbride, Gourock a Paisley, with arrivals from Carlisle and London. Fashic are much more casual, with not a hat in sight!

In modern times the queues on Fair Weekend a mostly found at **Glasgow Airport**, as folk leave fo place in the sun — Spanish resorts being the favour Gone is the camaraderie and anticipation of pleasu ahead — today's seasoned travellers look pretty bo with the whole business!

Housing and Health

ANNAN OG256

Thomas Annan's commission for the City of Glasgow Improvements Trust was to record the 'Old Closes and Streets' around Glasgow Cross. These had become an affront to the city fathers and were shortly to be demolished. The original houses of merchants and manufacturers had been colonised by workers, mostly immigrant Irish and Highlanders drawn to the prospects of jobs in the city's east end. Textiles, chemicals and iron foundries were all magnets to the victims of the potato famines of the 1840s. The subdivisions of the old houses resulted in terrible overcrowding and appalling living conditions. What according to Daniel Defoe had been 'one of the cleanliest, most beautiful and best-built cities in Great Britain' now accomodated five times as many people as it had a century earlier. This view of **80 High Street** (the Pawn Close, cf. p. 7) illustrates the problem.

Although the house is supplied with running water (n the jaw-box outside the first-floor window and dra pipes) the overcrowding was such that many famil had to use the one tap. The open drain in the close wo be for all fluid waste products, the solid material be collected by dustmen, nicknamed 'Midianites', from dry closets further along the close or in the dunnie (foundations). Many of the houses were 'ticketed' by Sanitary Department allocating 300 cubic feet per ac and 150 cu. ft for children, but most of these houses l additional 'lodgers' who hid in dunnies and ashpits wl the inspector's visit was due. It was printer's son Jc Blackie, then Lord Provost, who introduced the C Improvements Bill which was to remove the worst slu in Europe.

116

The City Improvements Trust replaced the mix of mills, workshops and workers' houses with purpose-built tenements, many of them room and kitchen and single-ends, with communal closets on the half-landing added later. A century afterwards Glasgow again faced the prospect of slum clearance, this time south of the river in Gorbals. The legend of the Gorbals was larger than life — many sound tenements were swept away in the enthusiasm of renewal, as much to purge the label as to improve living conditions. The Hutchesontown-Gorbals Comprehensive Development Area was then (1957) the largest in the UK. The first three schemes were completed in 1965; two more in 1970 to much fanfare and royal visit. And who could doubt that the **views from the new flats** (below) were breathtaking. After this, cost-cutting exercises were introduced which, in the long run proved expensive. The **Hutcheson-E** development of 756 flats built in 1973 had to be demolished in 1987, and others, including Sir Basil Spence's Queen Elizabeth Square, may suffer the same fate. Antipathy to soul-less monoliths has swung the planners to favour area rehabilitation and many Glasgow tenements are now being retained and improved.

STEWART SHAW

East End

Not all old houses in the east end were slums as this row of early **Calton cottages** shows. The brick walls are white-washed with lime and the washing is being brought out to the line, indicating the possibility of water somewhere within the house — perhaps at the top of the stairs with the plumbing down-pipes at the back of the closet under the stair. This pattern of house was copied on a grander scale for railway workers' houses at Cowlairs and Corkerhill. **Tenements** built for the C of Glasgow Improvements Trust were mainly of the ty found **in Balmano Brae** — four storeys, often with sho on the ground floor and a central close leading to t stair, with three houses on each landing, two of 'Roc and Kitchen' flanking a 'Single End'. After 1892 W were incorporated in the half-landing.

AC

Between the wars the Corporation bought tracts of agricultural land for the building of public housing on a grand scale. The early cottage-type developments at **Carntyne**, Riddrie, Mosspark and Knightswood were the most sought after, particularly by young people with families. It was hoped that as skilled workers moved into these new schemes their old houses could be occupied by folk from the slums which could then be demolished. This plan was too long-term and immediate relief schemes were built in Blackhill, Haghill, Possilpark and Govan. In the post-war era, twenty-nine Comprehensive Development Areas were outlined, covering one twelfth of the total city area. Through the 1960s and 70s a policy of high-rise developments was pursued as the solution to the housing problem, culminating in the notorious **Red Road flats** of thirty-one storeys. After fourteen years, two of the seven blocks were declared unfit for habitation, and the rest were converted to student residences and YMCA flats.

STEWART SHAW

Out West

Housing in the west end of Glasgow w
altogether different. Wealthy bu
nessmen sought country living for the
families and one railway company offere
them free first-class travel for five yea
from its new station at Lenzie. Bearsde
Kilmacolm and Helensburgh flourished
commuter villages about the same tim
Others preferred to be within a reaso
able carriage drive to town, and boug
dwellings among the splendid terrac
along the toll road from Anniesland to
George's Cross. **Great Western Terrac**
Alexander Thomson's last masterpiece,
probably the grandest of them all. S
William Burrell lived at Number VI
before retiring to Hutton Castle.

Gracious flats and the sandstone te
races of Sauchiehall Street, Woodlan
and **Hillhead** were the houses sought
the middle classes and profession
people. In Hillhead famous artists, arc
tects and academics are listed in the stre
directories. It is said that Hillhead still h
the highest IQ of any parliamenta
constituency in the country!

p management with families are
ll attracted to residences out of
wn, such as those built by Lovell
Redclyffe in Helensburgh. Sited
ose to Mackintosh's Hill House,
signed for William Blackie the
asgow publisher, Lovell spon-
red a competition among students
Glasgow School of Art for designs
stained glass door panels in the
RM tradition.

Today's middle-classes are
racted to flats nearer the centre of
wn, where old mills and ware-
uses have been converted or
built as amenity housing.
pecially attractive are the water-
nt developments at **Spiers Wharf**
d Carrick Quay.

LOVELL

F. LYALL

ANNAN OG274

GUL

The **Royal Infirmary** was first proposed by Geor[ge]
Jardine, Professor of Logic at the University, in 1787. [He]
obtained a royal charter from George III and rais[ed]
money by voluntary subscription to build the infirma[ry]
which was designed by Robert and James Adam. It co[n]
sisted of three blocks. The earliest, north of Cathed[ral]
Square, was finished in 1793. There was accommodati[on]
for 550 patients, half of these in the fever block.

Joseph Lister's appointment to the Chair of Surge[ry]
at the University coincided with the opening of the ne[w]
surgical block in 1860. He set out to prove that m[ost]
deaths after surgery occurred through bad hygiene a[nd]
not from 'influence of the atmosphere'. He showed [by]
steeping silk thread in weak carbolic acid that the pre[s]
ence of sutures did not set up infection. He cited his ea[rly]
experiments on a horse at the Vet College and on a la[d]
with an aneurism of the femoral artery who was up a[nd]
about six weeks after surgery.

Professor Robertson and his staff were pho[to]
graphed by William Graham c. 1898. Note the leg o'm[ut]
ton sleeves and wasp waistlines of the nursing staff [—]
the doctors too have a certain sartorial elegance!

The design competition for the second Glasgow Ro[yal]
Infirmary was won by James Miller in 1901, but t[he]
planned building aroused much protest because of [its]
size vis-a-vis the Cathedral. The south-facing Jubil[ee]
block was completed in 1914. The **modern Queen Eliz[a]
beth Building**, designed by Sir Basil Spence, Glov[er]
and Ferguson, lying north and east of the Miller Infirma[ry]
is the first (1986) phase of a complete Infirmary rebuil[d]
ing programme.

The **Waiting Room in the new Royal Infirmary c. 1911** shows health care then knew no social barriers. East end 'shawlie wifies' sit next to dowagers in furs and hats, whose body language indicates they are definitely 'not amused' by the presence of the photographer. If the patients were too ill to attend 'Out-Patients' they would be brought to hospital by vehicles belonging to the **St Andrew's Ambulance Association**, which held the franchise in Glasgow until 1948.

In modern times scientific advances are such that, if necessary, the medical team can operate away from the hospital and give more immediate relief to accident victims such as this case arriving by helicopter at the **Southern General Hospital**.

Education

The Scottish Education Act of 1872 brought parish and burgh schools under the control of School Boards and made education compulsory for all up to the age of thirteen. This was especially important for girls, since it was reckoned that twenty-five percent of females in the city were illiterate.

Besides the sixty-seven co-educational local author schools established by 1893, private educational esta lishments flourished. This class of **young ladies c. 18** was photographed by Wohlgemuth & Co. Sixty yea later T&R Annan photographed these pupils from t **Glasgow High School for Girls**.

SRA

'Up before the Heid' in 1886 looks a pretty awesome business. This family are being interviewed for places in **Green Street Day Industrial School**.

STEWART SHAW

Today children at **St Mark's Primary School** find school a fun place to be, and the work looks impressive too!

Glasgow University

Higher education in Glasgow started with
foundation of the University following a pet
to Pope Nicholas V in 1451 by William Turn
the Bishop of Glasgow. For three hund
years the old College taught mainly Divi
Arts and Law on a site south of the Cathec
The eighteenth century saw a blossomin
subjects on all fronts, particularly in scie
and medicine. One graduate, William Hur
bequeathed £8,000 together with his pri
collection which the University housed
museum designed by William Stark in
and photographed by GWW in 1868. W
the old College buildings were demolishe
1870, the collection, valued then at £130
was transferred to a new Hunterian Museu
Gilmorehill. The **old mansion of Gilmore**
was left standing in what is now the West Q
rangle as the University buildings rose ro
it. The former Hydropathic was used by
architect and contractors until 1872.

GWW F1068

GR

GWW E4556

The **University** remained **without its steeple** until a bequest by Andrew Cunningham permitted Gilbert Scott's son to finish the tower in 1888. in 1892 the University admitted women from Queen Margaret College to classes — about 350 women to 1700 men students by 1900.

The twentieth century buildings on the north side of University Avenue reflect the wide variety of disciplines pursued and the increased provision of library and refectory accommodation for students. The pre-war **reading room** sits next to the **new Library and Hunterian Museum**. The latter holds the best collection of Whistler paintings this side of the Atlantic, and a reconstruction of C.R. Mackintosh's house in Southpark Avenue.

STEWART SHAW

129

Anderson's College

The **Andersonian University** was founded under the will of John Anderson, Professor of Natural Philosophy in the University of Glasgow. 'Jolly Jack Phosphorous' strongly disagreed with the teaching methods of his employing institution and wished the new University 'to be open to all classes and both sexes'. In spite of lack of funds, the Trustees were able to offer evening classes in physics and chemistry in the old Grammar School, later to become the High School. From these classes sprang the Mechanics' Institute, which was copied nation-wide. Through several mergers the college was renamed the Royal College of Science and Technology, at which time the original building was replaced by the present sandstone one. Close links with industry were reflected in the core of subjects offered, even to separate lectureships in Dyeing and Bleaching and in Sugar Manufacturing. The Medical School had earlier moved to a site near the Western Infirmary and became part of the university in 1947. A further merger with the Scottish College of Commerce occurred before the Royal College acquired University status in 1964 as Strathclyde University.

All these historical strands explain the breadth of courses offered by **Strathclyde University** to its 8,000 students. The campus reflects the University's comparative youth with many striking buildings, such as the Wolfson Centre for Bio-Engineering (1971).

Glasgow School of Art

The **Glasgow School of Art** and Haldane Academy moved to its present famous building from the McLellan Galleries in 1899. A competition for the design had been won, perhaps through the influence of the Director, Francis Newbery, by a former student, Charles Rennie Mackintosh. The building was to have been funded by profits from the 1888 International Exhibition, but the Art Gallery and Museum, also a beneficiary, was built wildly over budget (£257,000) and the Art School design was thus limited to £14,000, to be built in two stages. East from Dalhousie Street up to and including the entrance was completed in 1899, but Mackintosh as only a draughtsman with Honeyman and Keppie, was not invited to the opening ceremony. The western half to Scott Street including the famous **Library** was completed ten years later.

trathclyde University

STEWART SHAW

University of Strathclyde
THE WOLFSON CENTRE

ROBERT BURNS

GDC

Today the School of Art still acts as a catalyst for modern 'Toshies', offering varied courses in painting, sculpture, design and architecture, the latter in conjunction with the University of Strathclyde. The School has many famous names among its graduates:, Sir David Murray, Sir John Lavery, Sir J. J. Burnet and George Henry of earlier years, and more recently Ken Currie, Steven Campbell, Liz Lochhead, Stephen Conroy, **Robbie Coltrane** and **Alasdair Gray**.

Charities, Rectorials, Graduations

COURTESY MRS M. MACKINNON

Charities week traditionally in January used to be an integral part of a student's education. These demure ladies in genuine 'ethnic' costume asked Glasgow to 'geisamoa' — a hard task **in 1930**. In recent times the novelty of 'letting your hair down' has gone, perhaps because some students look like it's rag week all year round! Local charities are less fashionable than other causes such as apartheid and the environment.

COURTESY MRS M. MACKINNON

At Glasgow University **Annie Macdonald MacKinnon graduated M.A. in 1932**. She taught in Skye and Invergarry before her marriage. Her three children are also University graduates in Arts and Medicine.

ectorial elections were a more serious matter alto-
ether though not without a history of mischief and skul-
uggery! The choosing of a man to represent them in
e corridors of power, was also the students' chance to
nour a famous graduate or local hero. Rivalry among
ndidates could reach fever pitch. 'Ygorra' was sung
th much vigour sometimes accompanied by missiles
infinite mess. Poets and politicians were favourites last
ntury, among them Thomas Campbell, a graduate and
thor of such poems as 'Lord Ullin's daughter' and
e Mariners of England'. He must have had enormous
arisma for he was elected Rector three times, beating
Walter Scott on one occasion. In the 1880s Disraeli
d Gladstone were both elected by Glasgow students,
t Rab Butler, victim of flour bombs at his installation
1958, must have thought the honour a doubtful one.
1990 pop beat politics into second place. Pat Kane,
nours graduate in English of 1985, but now singer with
e pop group Hue and Cry, was elected Rector. Tony
nn, doyen of the Labour Party and George Inglis,
mer student, were the other candidates.
At Strathclyde University, **Derek Alexander Ritchie**
aduated B.Sc. with first class honours in Technology
d Business Studies **in 1989**. He is now a supply analyst
th Mobil UK.

The earliest trams in the city were run by the **Glasgow Tramway and Omnibus Company** which leased track from Glasgow Corporation in 1872. None of the routes exceeded three miles and all radiated from the town centre. Tickets were colour coded, the dearest 3d ticket being a small boy's 'collectors' item'! There were fare stations, but no regulation stopping places. The driver stopped when waved to do so, though most gentlemen were adept at boarding 'on the move'. The trams held about thirty-six passengers.

In 1894 the **Corporation** did not renew the Company's lease and ran the system itself. Many fares were reduced by half, permitting even the poorest people to live further from work. By 1902 horsepower had been replaced by electricity serviced from the newly opened Pinkston Power Station, and colours as well as name-boards identified the routes. In 1962 trams were deemed to be the cause of traffic congestion and accidents, and many a penny was bent under that **last tram from Dalmuir West to Auchenshuggle**.

JAMAICA STREET, GLASGOW. 11,616. G.W.W.

STEWART SHAW

The earliest horse-drawn buses ran between the harbour at the Broomielaw to the canals at Port Dundas and Port Eglinton. In 1849 Andrew Menzies started a city and suburban service with tartan painted buses which persisted down to 1872, when he formed the Glasgow Tramway and Omnibus Company. The **three-horse buses** pictured in Jamaica Street look an exciting way to travel though only in fine weather! ↵

With the perfection of the internal combustion engine, buses enjoyed a freedom of route denied to the tram. The small **single-decker buses** photographed in Carlton Place c. 1920 were a 'Pullman' service operated by William J. Wright to Barrhead, Neilstone, Dunlop and Kilmarnock. Electrified trolley-buses were tried in the period 1949–67. The days of 'Come on, ge'raff' from clippies vanished when open rear-platform Corporation buses were replaced by **driver-operated, exact fare models**. The deregulation of local bus services in 1986 permitted independent companies to operate on Strathclyde Region's traditional routes and vice-versa resulting in some improvement of services in outlying areas but total chaos in the town centre.

By Under-ground

STEWART SHAW

On 11 April 1990 **the Underground** celebrated the tenth anniversary of its re-opening in new livery as Glasgow's 'clockwork orange'. The earlier Glasgow District Subway which it replaced took five years to build and ran carriages pulled by steam-driven cable until 1935. Thereafter electrical traction was used till 1977, when the new rolling-stock was introduced and the stations tiled squeaky clean.

ANNAN OG229

GWW A2239

DOULTON FOUNTAIN, THE GREEN, GLASGOW.   10,441.   G.W.W.

Glasgow Green was gifted by Bishop Turnbull to the people of Glasgow c. 1450 for common grazing land. From 1815 to 1826 James Clelland, Superintendent of Public Works, upgraded and improved the Green. The Molendinar and Camlachie Burns were culverted and Fleshers' Haugh drained. Walks were laid out and trees planted with a wide ride-and-drive carriage way, the latter for use mainly by subscribers. The Green's proximity to Glasgow's congested east end made it especially dear to the working class population, who used its public wash houses for almost a century, before they were removed to Greenhead Street, c. 1878.

The monument to Lord Nelson was raised just a year after he had been killed at Trafalgar in 1805, but it was damaged by lightning in 1810 and only then was it fitted with a lightning conductor! A similar fate befell the Statue of Queen Victoria atop the **Doulton Fountain**. It had been built for the 1888 International Exhibition in Kelvingrove Park, thereafter gifted to the city by the Doulton Company and removed to the Green in 1890. A year later the red terracotta statue was destroyed. There was some delay about her replacement and the Annan view of the Green was taken before this occurred.

St Andrew's Suspension Bridge was built in 1855 to replace a ferry joining the communities of Hutchesontown and Calton. Templeton's carpet factory, ornate and in the style of the Doge's Palace in Venice, reflected the prestigious nature of all developments along the north edge of the Green. Monteith Row, laid out by architect David Hamilton, was nicknamed 'Doctor's Row', and David Dale (father of the Scottish cotton industry) chose a house on the corner of Charlotte Street facing the Green.

OSCAR MARZAROLI

The Green has always been the venue for fun, epecially around the Fair in July when circus and semi-permanent buildings were erected. All seemed to suffer the same fate. Anderson's City Theatre was burned to the ground in 1845, as was Miller's building three years later. More enduring has been the People's Palace and wintergardens, opened in 1898. The aim was to provide under one roof a museum, picture-gallery, wintergarden and music hall for the working classes of the east end. It survives today but with long periods of neglect threats of closure have only been staved off by fierce support from staff and local people. Friends of the People's Palace have provided much needed visitor facilities and more extensions for 1990 will ensure the Palace's viability for many years to come.

In 1989 and 1990 the Green saw a new boom in open air concerts. The Glasgow group Wet, Wet, Wet staged a free 'gig' on September 10, 1989 to which 100,000 young people came, and a similar event was staged in June 1990.

For some the Green has been more important as a regular political meeting place. The Calton weavers demonstrated here in 1787 resulting in new barracks for 1000 soldiers being built in Gallowgate to bring law and order to bear on any similar situation. In the 19th Century great demonstrations preceded the Reform Bills of 1832, 1867 and 1884. Most memorable in recent times was the **UCS demonstration of 1971**. Politicians and pop-stars joined the shop-stewards in an amazing march which ended in Glasgow Green. Billy Connolly and Matt McGinn were among those helping to keep spirits high between the speeches.

The influence of James Cleland in smartening up Glasgow Green was an important one in the creation of more parks in the rest of the city. This had the further effect of desirable suburbs growing on their fringes. **The Botanic Gardens**, founded in 1817, were moved from the western end of Sauchiehall Street in 1839, but remained a private institution linked to the university until 1887. The giant Kibble Palace was reassembled in

the gardens from Kibble's home in Coulport in 1873 as a leafy palace of art and concert hall (there was a sunken orchestra pit under the central dome). Some 1500 people were invited to a private viewing prior to its opening to the public. Glasgow Corporation took possession as creditors in 1887 when funds ran out. Since that time they have tried to maintain the Gardens in the tradition of their founder, Thomas Hopkirk.

It seems only Grannie is interested in the paintings for sale in the **Botanic Gardens, 1958**. Children of every age prefer hoops and walls to sculpture and modern art!

Museums and the Arts

GWW E3601

GR

142

The first museum in the West End Park was housed in the eighteenth century mansion of **Kelvingrove House**. The grounds had been purchased in 1852 for the new park and the mansion was converted into an industrial museum for the city in 1871. There was also an aquarium and galleries of natural history and miscellaneous curiosities gifted by well-meaning patrons. When the new Art Gallery and Museum was completed the old museum was demolished to clear space for the 1901 Exhibition Concert Hall, though part of it was reprieved to house the Japanese Pavilion.

The **first Kelvin Hall** built as permanent exhibition space was burned down in July 1925. Its replacement was opened by King George V two years later on 12th July 1927. Many regular trade shows such as the Motor Show and the Ideal Homes Exhibition were held here besides the annual Christmas Carnival and Circus. In 1988 it reopened as the **Museum of Transport** (below) and an international sports arena, its function as an exhibition venue having been superseded by the new Scottish Exhibition Centre.

By far the most important addition to the museums of Glasgow has been the long-awaited home for the **Burrell Collection in Pollock Country Park**. Sir William Burrell, shipping magnate and art connisseur, left his collection to the city, provided that it was housed at least sixteen miles from the centre of town to avoid the city's polluted atmosphere. The Clean Air Act of 1956 enabled the Corporation to choose a parkland setting within the city boundary and still comply with the spirit of the bequest. The Museum was opened by the Queen in 1983 and now vies with Edinburgh Castle for first place in the tourist popularity stakes.

STEWART SHAW

STEWART SHAW

(ANNAN) AC

GR

Theatres and Concerts

Theatres in Glasgow in the Nineteenth Century all seemed doomed to the same fate — FIRE! The **Theatre Royal in Dunlop Street** was no exception. This Annan photograph was taken just before it was destroyed on the last night of the pantomime 'Blue Beard' in 1863. William Glover, son of the theatre's manager, transferred the royal patent to another theatre in Cowcaddens. It too was burned down in 1879. The **musical evening at Gryffe Castle in 1886** illustrates well the Victorian love of family entertainment. Charades and amateur dramatics were also popular. In 1948 these schoolgirls tried their hand at acting in **'Dorothy and the Apple-Pip'** preparing perhaps for future roles as an MP, deputy headteacher and academic! In 1990 an entirely professional performance was given by **Lulu**, Glasgow's own Eastender, who entertained the crowds in George Square at Glasgow's Hogmanay Party to welcome the start of the year of the City of Culture.

(ANNAN) AC

DAVID MITCHELL FOR GDC

'Memoirs and Portraits of Glasgow Men'

When Thomas Annan illustrated the *'Memoirs and Portraits of One Hundred Glasgow Men'* he was demonstrating his skills in the photogravure process, the British rights to which he had recently acquired. The publishers, John Maclehose & Sons, saw it as a natural sequel to their earlier partnership in *'The Old Country Houses of the Old Glasgow Gentry'*. But Annan was following a pattern established by G.W. Wilson some twenty years earlier with his *'Aberdeen Portraits'*. Both photographers used their stock of existing portraits of famous men, but Annan limited his choice to those who had 'died during the last thirty years and in their lives did much to make the city what it is.' This disposed of the delicate problem of whom to include from among his patrons who were still alive! Many Annan chose are now forgotten and sadly no women were included in the original collection.

The following leading lights reflect Annan's selections from church, town and gown, industry commerce and trade, media theatre and the arts.

1. **David Livingstone**, MD, LLD, was a Blantyre cotton worker who educated himself at night school and later at the Andersonian University to become a medical missionary. He earned his reputation as an explorer by his epic journey from the Zambezi to the Congo in 1854-6, his expedition up the Zambezi in 1858-64, and his search in Northern Tanganyika (1864-74) for the source of the Nile. During his second furlough the Livingstones lived next door to Talbot Cottage, Thomas Annan's home in Hamilton. The two were good friends and interesting photographs of the children of the two families survive from this period as well as this most famous portrait taken in 1864. [T. ANNAN]

2. **Archbishop Charles Petre Eyre** — born York, 1817, became a priest of the Roman Catholic Church in 1842 and, after service in various border parishes and the publication of a History of St Cuthbert, was nominated apostolic delegate in Scotland and titular bishop of Anazarbus, 1868. On the restoration of the Catholic hierarchy in Scotland he was translated to the archdiocese of Glasgow in 1878 and died there in 1902. [CPO]

3. **Norman MacLeod**, DD, popular preacher and minister of the Barony Church, 1851-72. Called 'the Great Norman' by his people, a writer and editor of church and other literature, he was appointed Chaplain to the Queen in 1860. His ministry attracted large numbers of Highlanders to his congregation, necessitating the building of a much larger church after his death in 1872. He was one of Annan's original Hundred Glasgow Men. [T. ANNAN–GUL]

4. **William Thomson**, Lord Kelvin, PC, OM, GCVO, MA, LLD, DCL, DSc, MD, FRS, DL, was born in Belfast in 1824, the son of James Thomson Professor of Mathematics at Glasgow University. William was a student and later Professor of Natural Philosophy at the Old College from 1846 to 1899. He was a very practical academic, and as consultant electrical engineer for the Atlantic cable invented the mirror galvanometer and siphon recorder. He also invented a mariners' compass and other electrical navigation instruments. He was created Lord Kelvin in 1892. He was Chancellor of the University of Glasgow from 1904 until his death in 1907. He is buried in Westminster Abbey beside Sir Isaac Newton and Charles Darwin. [GR]

5. **John Logie Baird** was born in Helensburgh in 1888. He spent five years at the Royal College of Science and Technology and Glasgow University. He took out more than 170 patents in his lifetime. His first and only commercial success was the 'Baird Undersock' an early thermal sock selling at 9d a pair! He is best known for his experiments with light in an effort to invent a method of 'seeing by wireless' — television. In spite of his being first to transmit colour and to develop photovision (an early form of video recording), the later electronic system of EMI-Marconi, using cathode ray tubes was deemed better. The outbreak of World War II prevented him perfecting the Baird Televisor, a high definition colour system, and he died aged 58 without fame or fortune. [SU–CG]

6. **Sir William Bilsland**, JP, LLD, (1847-1921) was Lord Provost of Glasgow and Lord Lieutenant of the County of the City of Glasgow between 1905 and 1908, having served as Councillor for the Anderston Ward from 1886. Dubbed 'the successful scone grocer' by Petrie the Glasgow 'Clincher', he was chairman of Bilsland Brothers, the bakery chain whose giant factory dominated Hydepark Street from 1882. He played a leading role in the provision of health care for the poor in the city and was knighted in 1907. [J. C. ANNAN–GR]

7. **Sir William Arrol**, LLD, FRSE, DL (1839-1913), head of the engineering firm in Bridgeton which built many famous bridges including the Tay and Forth railway bridges, Tower Bridge and the Forth and Humber road bridges. He was Member of Parliament for South Ayrshire 1895-1906, and a director of Fairfield Shipbuilding and Engineering Co. [GR]

8. **Walter Montgomery Neilson**, locomotive builder, whose Hyde Park Works in Springburn (1860) set the pattern for subsequent development in the area. He was son of John Neilson, inventor of the hot-blast furnace. [S&T]

9. **Robert Napier** (1791-1876), marine engineer and shipbuilder, whose works at Lancefield and Govan built many of the famous ships associated with the Clyde, such as Persia and the Black Prince. his yards were a training ground for other future competitors. [SRA]

10. **Sir William Burrell** (1861-1958), shipping magnate, town councillor and art connoisseur. He was an organiser of the 1901 International Exhibition and lent more than two hundred pieces to be exhibited — a foretaste of the gift of his magnificent collection to the city in 1944. [GAG&M–BC]

11. **James Pagan**, journalist, succeeded George Outram as Editor of the Glasgow Herald in 1856. He introduced new ways of reporting, turned the Glasgow Herald into a daily paper and developed the leading article on subjects of local, historical and topographic interest. He wrote a number of pamphlets and books including a *Sketch of the History of Glasgow* (1847). [GR]

12. **John Buchan**, JP, LLD, DL, (1875-1940) was first Baron Tweedsmuir and author of over fifty books. Son of the Free Church minister of John Knox Church, Gorbals, he attended Hutcheson Grammar and Glasgow University before distinguishing himself at Oxford and in his subsequent diplomatic career. He was appointed Governor General of Canada in 1935. He is best remembered now for his adventure novels. [SRA]

13. **Neil Munro**, LLD, (1864-1930), author and Editor of the Glasgow Evening News, was born in Inverary and used his Highland background as setting for many of his novels such as *'John Splendid'*. His fondness for the Clyde and steam puffers were immortalised in his tales of Para Handy, which have since been revived through film and television. His autobiographical account of life in Edwardian Glasgow is recorded in *'The Brave Days'*. [GH]

14. **John Henry Anderson** (1814-74) hailed from Aberdeen and thus used the title 'Wizard of the North'. He was a showman whose genius for publicity made him several fortunes in his lifetime. He built the Glasgow City Theatre in 1845 to realise his ambition of actor/manager playing to houses of 5000. The dream turned to ashes when the theatre burned down. As a member of the Garrick Club, Anderson gave numerous benefit shows for public institutions and charities. A second fire, this time in London's Covent Garden theatre, reduced the Wizard to penury. He performed before royalty including Tzar Nicholas I and Queen Victoria at Balmoral. The portrait by GWW taken in 1854 is an early collodion-calotype. [ACAD]

15. **Harry Gordon**, another Aberdonian, also took his north humour to Glasgow to win fame and fortune. As the 'Laird of Inversnecky', he retained enough Doric to be individual while also being understood by lowland Scots. He often played Dame in pantomime to Will Fyffe's male comic, notably in the Alhambra during the War. He wrote most of his own material, including the sentimental song *'Down in the Glen'*. He died in 1959. [GH]

16. **Will Fyffe** was a straight actor turned comic. A Dundonian by birth, he wrote and made famous 'I belong to Glasgow'. Many of his spoonerisms have become part of Glasgow patter — 'I may be under the affluence of inkohol, but I'm not so think as you drunk I am.' He was popular in the USA and made many films there. [GH]

17. **James Bridie** (1888-1951), CBA, MD, LLD, ChB, FRCPS, was born Osborne Henry Mavor. Educated at Glasgow Academy and the High School, he studied medicine at Glasgow University and was a practising physician and surgeon until 1938. He is more widely known by his pseudonym for plays such as *'The Anatomist'*, *'Tobias and the Angel'* and *'Dr Angelus'*. With Tom Honeyman and others he was a strong supporter of local repertory theatres, culminating in the founding of the Glasgow Citizens' Theatre in 1942. [GH]

18. **George Henry**, a member of the Glasgow School, best remembered for his use of vivid colour (cf. 'Galloway Landscape' in Glasgow Art Gallery). With E. A. Hornell he pioneered collaborative works such as 'The Druids' and 'The Star in the East', collaboration becoming a feature of the 'Glasgow Boys' group of artists. These companion pieces are said to have influenced those who were to develop the 'Glasgow Style' which blossomed a decade later. [J. C. ANNAN]

19. **Catherine Cranston** was a member of the family which owned the Crow Hotel in George Square and smoke and tea rooms in Argyle Street and Buchanan Street. Her key to success lay in providing restaurants where ladies could go unaccompanied She married Major John Cochrane and together they became patrons of C. R. Mackintosh, having him decorate and furnish their home, as well as new tearooms in Buchanan Street, Ingram Street and Sauchiehall Street. [J. C. ANNAN]

20. **Charles Rennie Mackintosh** (1868-1928) was educated at Allan Glen's School and the School of Art. He joined the firm of Honeyman and Keppie and in 1889 won the Alexander Thomson travelling Scholarship which financed an Italian tour in 1891. Together with Herbert MacNair and the Macdonald sisters, Margaret (whom he married) and Frances, he established the Glasgow Style which has had a late 20th century revival.
Mackintosh designed the Glasgow Herald building, Martyr's Public School, Queen Margaret's Medical College , Queen's Cross Church, Glasgow School of Art and Scotland Street School. Independent commissions from prominent Glaswegians included Windyhill, Kilmacolm and Hill House, Helensburgh, as well as the Cranston Tearooms. The Mackintoshes exhibited abroad to wide acclaim, but in Scotland their efforts were treated with indifference. In 1913 he resigned from Honeyman and Keppie and spent most of his later years in France. [J. C. ANNAN]

1. **William Barclay**, OBE, DD, was a popular preacher and teacher. He was a missionary to the masses as well as Professor of Divinity and Biblical Criticism at the University of Glasgow. Over sixty of his books are still in print. His *'Daily Study Bible'* and a translation of the New Testament into every-day English made the Bible live. He was an enthusiastic conductor of University and church choirs and his honorary positions with the YMCA and the Boys' Brigade reflected the breadth of his interest in other areas of Christian service. He died in 1978.

2. **William Morris**, JP, LLD, DD, a Welshman, has been Minister of Glasgow Cathedral since 1967. Made a Chaplain to the Queen in Scotland in 1969, he also serves as Chaplain to many Glasgow organisations including Strathclyde Police and the YMCA. He has been responsible for maintaining the Cathedral as a place of worship, not just a tourist attraction. [GH]

3. **Archbishop Thomas Winning**, DD, a Wishaw man, was ordained as priest in 1948 and served in Lanarkshire and the Scots college in Rome before becoming parish priest in Motherwell and Clydebank. He was nominated titular bishop of Louth in 1971 and succeeded James Scanlan as Archbishop of Glasgow in 1974. He is an honorary fellow of the Educational Institute of Scotland. [CPO]

4. **Sir William Fraser**, GCB, LLD, FRSE, Principal of Glasgow University since 1988 is a graduate in Arts and Law of the University. His undergraduate experience as Secretary and President of the Students Representative Council might be seen as good training for his later career in the Scottish Office, latterly as Permanent Under-Secretary of State.

5. **Sir Graham Hills**, DSc, LLD, former Principal of Strathclyde University, graduated from Birkbeck College, London University, then lectured in Physical Chemistry at Imperial College, moving to the University of Southampton as Professor in 1962. He was a visiting Professor in Canada, the USA and Argentina, and has recently been appointed to the Board of the Glasgow Development Agency.

6. **Charles Oakley**, JP, BSc, MEd, CBIM, LLD, a Devon man, came to Glasgow to study marine engineering with John Brown's in Clydebank. He lectured at Aberdeen and Glasgow Universities on industrial psychology and was seconded to the Civil Service in 1930. After time in the Air Ministry, he became Scottish Controller for the Board of Trade. He was President of the Glasgow Chamber of Commerce 1966–7. An authority on the history of Glasgow, his most famous book, *'The Second City'*, is now in its fourth edition.

7. **Sir Norman Macfarlane**, LLD, since 1973 Chairman and Managing Director of Macfarlane Group (Clansman) Plc, a Scottish company manufacturing plastics etc for the computer and whisky industries. He is chairman and a director of many other important companies and financial institutions including the Glasgow Development Agency which, along with his patronage and help to the arts, brought a life peerage in 1991. He is Chairman of Governors of the High School (his old school) and an Honorary Vice-President of the Glasgow Battalion of the Boys' Brigade.

8. **Susan Baird**, JP, Lord Provost of the City of Glasgow since 1988 has represented the Parkhead Ward since 1974 and was elected a baillie of the city in 1980. She is only the second woman in Glasgow's history to hold the office of Lord Provost.

9. **Lord Fraser of Allander**, DL, LLD, JP, was Chairman and Managing Director of the House of Fraser 1941–64, and at different times chairman of John Barker, Harrods, Associated Fisheries, the Highland Tourist Development Co., and George Outram and Co. Though best remembered as the Glaswegian who bought Harrods, his last take-over fight to keep the Glasgow Herald in local hands won the more publicity. Through his Scottish and Universal Investment Company Sir Hugh defeated Lord Thomson of Fleet for control of the newspaper in October 1964, and became first Baron Fraser two months later. He died in 1966. [GH]

10. **Sir Eric Yarrow**, MBE, DL, Chairman of the Clydesdale Bank Plc and member of the Yarrow shipbuilding dynasty, has also served as director, managing director, chairman and now president of Yarrow's Plc. He is director of other financial institutions, Hon. President of the Princess Louise Scottish Hospital, Erskine, and Deputy Lieutenant of Renfrewshire.

11. **Arnold Kemp**, MA, an Edinburgh man who learned his craft with The Scotsman and The Guardian before being appointed Editor of the Glasgow Herald in 1981. He says he has survived the culture switch, and now leads his team of writers in their hi-tech home in Albion Street with his own blend of political panache and blue pencil.

12. **Jack House** who died in 1991, was a journalist and author of more than sixty-seven books mostly about Scotland and his native Glasgow. He worked in all three Glasgow evening newspapers, BBC radio and tv. He was awarded the St Mungo Prize for his services to the city. [GDC]

13. **James Gordon**, CBE, MA, Managing Director of Radio Clyde was a classics scholar and President of Glasgow University Union. He taught for five years before becoming a tv journalist and presenter. He was Political Editor with Scottish Television until 1973 before joining Radio Clyde.

14. **Jimmy Logan**, FRCMD, is a modern actor-manager who started as a child star as one of the Logan family. He starred in summer revues and pantomime and bought the New Metropole in 1964, mounting productions as diverse as *'Rob Roy'* and *'Hair'*. His recent memorable roles include *'Lauder'*, the archetypal Scot, and Englishman Archie Rice in *'The Entertainer'*. [GDC]

15/16. **Jack Milroy** and **Rikki Fulton** have distinguished careers in acting, music hall and tv — Jack in summer shows such as *'Whirl of Laughter'*, Rikki in straight and comic roles such as the Rev. I.M. Jolly, culminating in the TRICS President's Award for his contribution to broadcasting in 1987 and an OBE in 1991. Their Teddy-boy double act as Francie and Josie continues popular despite the disappearance of the type, and their unique chemistry keeps the King's Theatre fully booked when they appear. [GDC]

17. **Robbie Coltrane** trained at Glasgow School of Art but quickly moved into theatre, television and film. He is a character actor with a gift for comedy, as his 1990 one-man show *'Mistero Buffo'* exemplified. TV roles in *'Tutti Frutti'* and *'Blackadder'* and films such as *'Danny, Champion of the World'* and *'Nuns on the Run'* show this Scot excels abroad as well as at home. [GDC]

18. **Liz Lochhead**, Dip Art, DLitt, poet and dramatist, combined writing and art teaching for eight years before pursuing her writing full-time. Her first collection of poems was published in 1972. She is recognised for her modern dramas *'Now and Then'* and *'True Confesssions'*. She has been Writer-in-Residence with the Royal Shakespeare Company since 1989. [GH]

19. **Sir William Collins** was the fifth generation of his family to be head of the local firm of publishers and printers whose early prosperity was based on the printing of bibles and religious literature. He was the third of his family to be knighted for service to the community. 'Billy' is remembered as the man who made Collins an international firm, culminating in the move to the hi-tech plant at Bishopbriggs. The University of Strathclyde acquired the Collins buildings and land in Cathedral Street and the Collins Gallery in Richmond Street through Sir William's generous support. This was acknowledged in 1973 by the conferral of the honorary degree of LL.D. He died in 1976. [SU–CG]

20. **Barry Gasson** as an outsider is one who in Annan's words has done 'much to make the city what it is.' An architect in private practice, he also runs a biodynamic farm in Ayrshire and commutes to Manchester where he is a Visiting Professor. His design for the Galleries to hold the Burrell Collection in Pollock Park, has won many local and national wards, the most recent being the Gold Medal of the Fourth Bienniale of Architecture.

'I Belong to Glasgow'

Photographers . . .

Thomas Annan (1829–1887), the fifth son of a Fife farmer, came to Glasgow to work as a lithographer with Joseph Swan. He was a strong Free Church man and an admirer of the work of Hill and Adamson who were engaged in photographing the Free Church ministers for Hill's painting 'The Signing of the Deed of Demission, 1843'. In 1855 Annan set up as a collodion-calotypist in Woodlands Road, moving shortly to Sauchiehall Street. He sold scenic views and portraits, but his expertise lay in copying works of art. His early commissions from the Glasgow Art Union brought instant acclaim. In 1866 Annan was asked by Hill to reproduce the finished Disruption painting — 11 feet long — in various sizes for purchase by members of the new Church.

Annan also published volumes of views of *Glasgow Cathedral* (1867), *Glasgow* (1868) and *Days on the Coast* (1867), but it was the commission to photograph the *Old Closes and Streets* (1868) which secures his place in the history of photography. His subsequent illustrations of the Old Country Houses of the Old Glasgow Gentry (1870) and the *Memorials of the Old College of Glasgow* (1871) have less impact.

George Washington Wilson (1823–1893) was son of a Banffshire crofter. In Edinburgh he became a miniaturist and back in Aberdeen in 1848 offered his clients a choice in portraiture, though first using photography as a means to an end, as D. O. Hill did. Wilson also experimented with stereo views and a prosperous business began. His commission to photograph the rebuilding of Balmoral Castle was the start of a Royal patronage which lasted till his death. His business progressed on two fronts, portaiture and topographic views. He published his first one hundred *Aberdeen Portraits* in 1857 and eight other portrait groups were to follow. Wilson himself was more interested in his stereo and album views. These were published in a series titled *Photographs of English and Scottish Scenery*. He also illustrated the works of Sir Walter Scott and J.M. Barrie as well as the Queen's Journal, and received medals for his 'instantaneous' photography. GWW visited favourite cities time and again to record historic change. He liaised with Annan to use the carbon process, and it is thought that they bought each other's negatives to print locally. When GWW died his sons continued the business until 1907 when 65000 glass negatives were sold at auction. The bulk of these remained in local hands until gifted to the University of Aberdeen in 1954.

Although Thomas Annan had been joined by brother Robert in 1873, it was his sons, notably **James Craig Annan** (1864–1946), who were to carry on the photographic tradition. Thomas had been interested in different reproduction processes, securing the Scottish rights for carbon printing in 1866. After an apprenticeship alongside brother John in the new premises at Lenzie, and further study of chemistry, James accompanied his father Thomas to Vienna in 1883 to learn photogravure from its inventor Karl Klic. Together they secured the British rights for the new process and used it successfully in the *Memoirs and Portraits of One Hundred Glasgow Men* (1878). James became one of the Secessionist movement, which sought to pursue artistic excellence in the medium of photography, and was elected to the Ring Brotherhood in 1892. His portraits of famous people were most admired, and in 1900 was honoured by the inaugural one-man show mounted by the Royal Photographic Society. He subsequently participated in major exhibitions in London, Brussels, Paris, Vienna and New York, all the while continuing the more routine business of fine art photography in Glasgow.

William Graham (1845–1914) was born in Springburn and worked for most of his life as a railway man with the North British Railway Company. His hobby was photography, and he took many railway and technical photographs. In 1893, by which time he was an engine-driver, Graham supported a strike, after which he left (or was fired!). He chose to turn his hobby into a profession, setting up a studio in Vulcan Street. Graham was a founder member of the Old Glasgow Club, and recorded many of the city's historic buildings and churches. His portraits of Springburn people and local characters show a different side of Glasgow to that recorded by Annan. After his death Baillie Hepburn purchased the Graham collection of some 3000 glass negatives and presented it to the Mitchell Library.

GR

Oscar Marzaroli (1933–88) was born in Italy but brought up in Glasgow in Garnethill. He attended some courses at Glasgow School of Art before becoming a photographer's assistant. He worked in Stockholm and London as a photo-journalist then returned to Glasgow to his own 'Studio 59'. In 1961 he joined Templar Film Studios until in 1967 he founded Ogam Films with three friends. He continued to record on stills faces and places that caught his imagination, and returned to that work when the Ogam partnership was dissolved. His work has been widely exhibited and published, notably in *Shades of Grey* (1987) and *Shades of Scotland* (1989). A Trust (and an archive) now seeks to make his work more widely known.

© ANNE MARZAROLI

SARAH MACKAY

Stewart D. Shaw, CA, BSc, is a Dundonian who has worked in Glasgow since 1980. His interest in photography has slowly overtaken his professional life. He is a member of the Board of the Glasgow Photography Group, the parent organisation of Street Level, the new photographic gallery and workshop in High Street. He has exhibited in Glasgow and elsewhere and won a Glasgow District Council commission to photograph Turin, one of Glasgow's twin cities, as part of the Year of Culture 1990 programme.

Index

Select Bibliography

Thomas Annan: Photographs of Glasgow, 1868 (Dover ed. 1977); Old Closes and Streets of Glasgow, 1868–77; Old Country Houses of the Old Country Gentry, 1870; Memorials of the Old College of Glasgow, 1871; Memoirs and Portraits of One Hundred Glasgow Men, 1878.

William Barr, Glaswegiana, 1972.

Berry and H. Whyte, Glasgow Observed, 1987.

David Daiches, Glasgow, 1982.

Kenneth Davies, The Clyde Passenger Steamers, 1980.

James Denholm, The History of the City of Glasgow, 1798.

A. M. Doak and A. M. Young, Glasgow at a Glance, 1965, 1983.

William Graham (1845–1914), Glasgow Scrapbooks.

and I. Hackney, Charles Rennie Mackintosh, 1989.

Jack House, The Heart of Glasgow, 1965; Glasgow, Then and Now, 1974, 1988; Music Hall Memories, 1986.

Hume and T. Jackson, George Washington Wilson and Victorian Glasgow, 1983.

Hume and M. Moss, Clyde Shipbuilding from Old Photographs, 1975; Glasgow As It Was, vols. I & II, 1975, vol. III, 1976; Workshops of the British Empire, 1977; Beardmore — History of a Scottish Giant, 1979.

William Hunter, Dear Happy Ghosts, 1898–1990, Scenes from the Outram Archive, 1990.

Peter Kearney, The Glasgow Cludgie, 1985.

and J. Kinchin, Glasgow's Great Exhibitions, 1988.

Elspeth King, The People's Palace and Glasgow Green, 1985.

Maurice Lindsay, Portrait of Glasgow, 1972, 1981; Victorian and Edwardian Glasgow from Old Photographs, 1987.

C. McKean, D. Walker and F. Walker, Central Glasgow, 1989.

A. McLean, A North British Album, 1975; The Edinburgh and Glasgow Railway (forthcoming).

Andrew McQueen, Clyde River Steamers of the Last Fifty Years, 1924; Echoes of the Old Clyde Paddlesteamers, 1924.

Oscar Marzaroli and William McIlvanney, Shades of Grey — Glasgow 1956–87, 1987.

Alan Massie, Glasgow — Portraits of a City, 1989.

William Morris, A Walk through Glasgow's Cathedral, 1986.

Henry B. Morton, A Hillhead Album, 1973.

M. Nicholson and M. O'Neill, Glasgow: Locomotive Builder to the World, 1987.

Charles Oakley, Men at Work, 1946; The Second City, 1946, 1967, 1975, 1990; Our Industrious Forbears, 1982; The Last Tram, 1962.

James Pagan, Sketches of the History of Glasgow, 1847.

Alastair Phillips, Glasgow's Herald, 1783–1983, 1982.

Donald Saunders and others, The Glasgow Diary, 1984.

Aileen Stuart, Villages of Glasgow, 1988.

Sara Stevenson, Thomas Annan, 1829–87, 1990.

Frank Wordsall, The Glasgow Tenement, 1979, 1989; The City that Disappeared, 1991.

E. Williamson, A. Riches and M. Higgs, The Buildings of Scotland — Glasgow, 1990.

George Washington Wilson, Photographs of English and Scottish Scenery — Glasgow, 1868, 1870.

William Young, Glasgow Scrapbooks, 1878–1915.

Journals: Avenue (the Graduate Magazine of Glasgow University); British Journal of Photography; The Glasgow Herald; Journal — Glasgow Chamber of Commerce; Leopard Magazine (Aberdeen); Scottish Photography Bulletin; Transactions of the Old Glasgow Club, 1907–55.

Heather Lyall was born and brought up in Carntyne, educated at the Glasgow High School for Girls, and is a graduate of the Universities of Aberdeen and Glasgow. A cartography specialist, she has worked in the Departments of Geography in the Universities of Aberdeen, Budapest and Auckland. When her three children were older, she returned to academic life as a Research Assistant in Economic History in the University of Aberdeen and now holds a similar post in the History Department there. She worked on the series of books of George Washington Wilson photographs published by Aberdeen University Library and is the author of *Vanishing Aberdeen* (1988), the model for the current series. She is a member of the Scottish Society for the History of Photography.

Back Cover   Briggait (Annan) 'Ben More' (GWW)
                     'QE II' (OM) Glasgow's Miles Better (SS)